Osprey Modelling • 10

CW01024439

Modelling the Jagdpanzer 38(t) 'Hetzer'

Gary Edmundson

Consultant editor Robert Oehler

Series editors Marcus Cowper and Nikolai Bogdanovic

First published in Great Britain in 2004 by Osprey Publishing, Elms Court, Chapel Way, Botley, Oxford OX2 9LP, United Kingdom. Email: info@ospreypublishing.com

ISBN 1 84176 705 0

Editorial by Ilios Publishing, Oxford, UK (www.iliospublishing.com)
Design: Servis Filmsetting Ltd, Manchester, UK
Index by Alison Worthington
Originated by Global Graphics, Prague, Czech Republic
Printed and bound in China by L-Rex Printing Company Ltd

04 05 06 07 08   10 9 8 7 6 5 4 3 2 1

A CIP catalogue record for this book is available from the British Library.

FOR A CATALOGUE OF ALL BOOKS PUBLISHED BY OSPREY MILITARY AND AVIATION PLEASE CONTACT:

Osprey Direct UK, P.O. Box 140, Wellingborough,
Northants, NN8 2FA, UK
E-mail: info@ospreydirect.co.uk

Osprey Direct USA, c/o MBI Publishing, P.O. Box 1,
729 Prospect Ave, Osceola, WI 54020, USA
E-mail: info@ospreydirectusa.com

www.ospreypublishing.com

Author's note

I wish to acknowledge the following people for their help and generosity in preparing this book:

Freddie Leung of Dragon Models Ltd.
Kong Nam Industrial Building
10/FL, B1, 603-609 Castle Peak Road
Tsuen Wan, N.T., Hong Kong
Tel: (852) 2493 0215 Fax: (852) 2411 0587
www.dragon-models.com

Lutz Fellmuth of New Connection Models
Dorfgütingen 40
91555 Feuchtwangen
Germany
Tel: (49) 9852 4329
www.new-connection.de

Jim Johnston of Fort Duquesne Miniatures
105 Tristan Dr.
Pittsburgh
PA 15209
USA
Tel: (412) 486 1823 Fax: (412) 486 5217
Email: ftduq@stargate.net

François Verlinden of Verlinden Productions, Inc.
811 Lone Star Drive
O'Fallon, MO 63366
USA
Tel: (636) 379 0077
Fax: (636) 281 0011
www.verlinden-productions.com

I'd also like to thank my fellow modelling colleagues for their invaluable assistance, encouragement and support with this book: Jon Feenstra, Ed Kusiak, Ron Volstad and Tom Cockle

Editor's note

Contents

Introduction

The Jagdpanzer 38(t) 'Hetzer' was developed in the latter stages of World War II in an effort to make up for losses in assault-gun production due to the Allied bombing of German factories. A highly successful design, the little tank hunter was fast and relatively inexpensive to manufacture. Using proven components from the Panzer 38(t), it proved a valuable weapon on both the Eastern and Western fronts of the war with its potent 7.5cm Pak 39/L48 gun. Taking advantage of the factory facilities of BMM and Skoda in Czechoslovakia, the Germans produced over 2,500 vehicles of this type between April 1944 and May 1945. Soon after the war, the Swiss and Czech armies used modified versions of the Hetzer (designated G-13 and ST-1 respectively) up until the 1970s.

In the mid-1970s, the Italian manufacturer Italeri released the first 1/35-scale kit of the Jagdpanzer 38(t) 'Hetzer'. The kit represented the later version of the tank destroyer, produced in Autumn 1944. A fairly accurate model for its time, the kit was attractively packaged featuring the work of Belgian modeller François Verlinden. Verlinden's innovative AFV modelling showed that properly painted models could look quite realistic. This kit has also been marketed by Revell, and even found its way into Tamiya's product line in some Asian countries.

For the next two decades, the Italeri model stood alone until the Chinese manufacturer Dragon Models Ltd. (DML) began to produce a more state-of-the-art model in terms of accuracy and detail. Dragon have produced three kits of the Hetzer to date, with all of them featuring the DML standard of individual link tracks and etched-metal detail.

This guide to modelling the Hetzer uses the DML 1/35-scale models as a basis, and step-by-step guides on building an early and late version of the vehicle are presented. Two variants of the vehicle are also featured: the sIG 33, mounting the 15cm infantry gun, and the Bergepanzer 38(t) recovery vehicle. The section on the latter vehicle will concentrate on placing the model in a realistic setting. In researching this project, I had the opportunity to measure and photograph the Hetzer in Aberdeen, Maryland, USA, and am able to say that the DML kit is fairly accurate in dimension.

There were no clearly defined Ausführung, or model numbers, as the Hetzer developed from early to late. A series of modifications were introduced over the 13 months of its production during World War II and the technical details of

The author with the late Hetzer in Aberdeen, Maryland, in April 2003.

4

these modifications can be found in Osprey's New Vanguard 36 on the Hetzer. In addition to the basic model kits used, aftermarket products and other miscellaneous materials are incorporated to make the models as authentic and accurate as possible.

Each of the models depicted in this book incorporates modifications that accumulate with each successive chapter. To avoid repetition, detailed modifications dealt with in previous chapters will receive less attention in the successive builds. Some aspects of construction that require a certain emphasis may be reiterated in the photo captions.

The construction measurements for the models are given in millimetres. Since materials such as styrene sheet and tubing, and brass rod are generally sold in thousandths of an inch, their dimensions are given in imperial measurements.

The painting process for the models is described in the chapter on the sIG 33 version of the Hetzer. Although the colour scheme is specific to the sIG 33, the same techniques are used on all the models in this publication. Exceptions and additions regarding each of the other builds have been specified in 'Notes on painting and markings'.

DML's kit no. 6030, featured in both the early Hetzer and sIG 33 version models in this book. After going out of production, it was re-released in late 2002.

DML's kit no. 6037 was introduced soon after their release of the early version. Parts are included to make the flame-thrower version.

Materials

The following section describes the various tools and materials used in the construction and painting of the models. Although many of these items are quite general in regard to scale modelling, some of them were specifically acquired for use on this project.

Styrene sheet, rod and tubing

Several sheets of various thicknesses of styrene sheet were needed for the more challenging aspects of the model construction. Typical sizes used were .040in., .020in., .015in., .010in., and .005in. Where odd sizes were needed, sheets were laminated together with liquid glue. Many different sizes of styrene rod and tubing were used, purchased at a local model railway shop. Invaluable tools for working with styrene are a large straight-edge ruler to use as a cutting guide and a smaller ruler with millimetre and inch markings.

Punch and die set

Although expensive, this handy device helped with many of the parts such as the ammo stowage racks in the late Hetzer, spacers, washers and other details.

Chopper

The 'Chopper' is an excellent tool for getting an accurate cut repeated numerous times at an exact 90-degree angle. It was used extensively in the construction of the many leaf-spring assemblies and parts for the ammo stowage racks in the late Hetzer.

Soldering equipment for the etched-brass parts

Cyanoacrylate glue can be used to bond etched-brass parts together in most cases. However, for some of the bigger jobs, especially where strength is needed, the brass needs to be soldered together. The mudguards, jack mounts and stowage boxes were all put together using a small butane soldering pen.

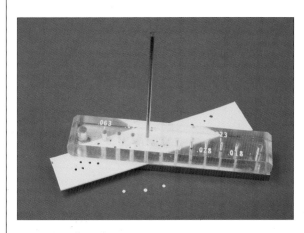

An invaluable tool used throughout the construction of the models in this book was a punch and die set from Waldron. Both the Precision and Sub-Miniature sets were used, with sizes ranging from .16in. to .018in.

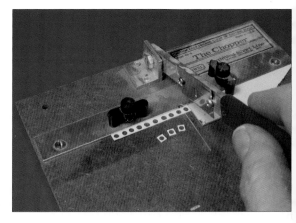

The Chopper, shown here making parts for the ammunition racks in the late Hetzer, handled cuts requiring accurate repetition. The base below can wear out after constant use, and was given new life with an epoxy putty repair.

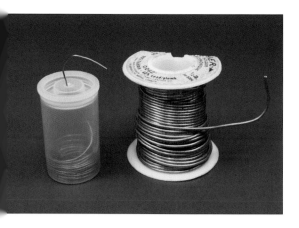

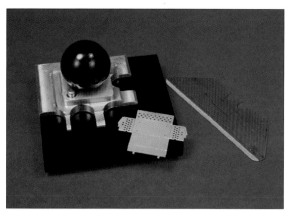

Lead wire and solder of various sizes is easily shaped and glued. It comes in very handy for wiring, conduits and other piping. It's also great for soldering!

Etched-metal benders have taken some of the frustration out of forming the brass pieces accurately. Available in various sizes, the smaller Hold & Fold is shown here. The 4in. version was needed to bend the rear mudguards on the Hetzers.

RTV Rubber moulds and resin casting

Resin parts were cast for some of the detail on the models. The idler wheels for the late Hetzer and Bergepanzer, as well as the radios for the late and sIG 33 versions were made from masters using RTV rubber moulds.

Etched-metal bender

To help bend the etched-brass parts a tool called 'Hold & Fold' was used. There are two different brands of this kind of device at the time of writing, sold in different sizes. The 4in. size was needed to work with the Hetzer's Aber mudguards.

Putty and glue

'Zimm-It-Rite' epoxy putty was most commonly used for this project since it's the best handling type I have found. Small details like seat cushions and weld beads were formed from this material, which dries rock hard overnight.

Tamiya's lacquer-based putty is an excellent medium for creating cast metal texture as well as filling gaps. Larger holes and gaps were filled with epoxy putty or styrene.

To help adhere the various plastic, resin and metal parts together I used what's commonly referred to as superglue, or 'cyano' for short. Styrene to styrene bonds were formed with Testor's liquid cement, which also works for resin to styrene bonds as well. Liquid cement also softens the styrene enough to stick to smaller brass parts for alignment, these were then fixed permanently with cyano glue.

Lead wire and foil

Sold as solder in hardware shops and fly-tying wire in fishing shops, hobby companies now carry various sizes of lead wire for detailing models. Conduits and wiring are easily formed and cemented using the various sizes available, .010in. and .020in. were used the most on these builds.

Lead foil can be purchased, or scavenged from tops of wine bottles. Its many uses include forming retaining straps, gun slings and conduit supports. The foil can also be obtained with an adhesive backing – used here to correct the sloppy fit of the wheels to the suspension arms.

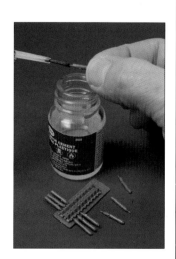

Testor's liquid cement is shown being used to construct the Model Kasten track runs. Other glues used in modelling the vehicles were cyano, or superglue, and PVA white glue. Although cyano was used to adhere some of the brass parts, soldering was used where a strong bond was required.

Airbrush and pressure supply

To obtain the finish quality and take advantage of the painting techniques described in this work an airbrush and pressure supply are essential. The

A single action Paasche H-1 airbrush was used for painting the models. With some exceptions, Tamiya was the paint of choice because of its fine spraying qualities when thinned out.

single-action airbrush used for these models is not elaborate, and the pressure supply is a noisy, bone-rattling Campbell & Hausfeld compressor with a 7-gallon tank and regulator.

Paints

Various types of paint were used to finish the models in this publication. Each one has a unique advantage for the situation in which they are used. In summary, Tamiya and Model Master acrylic paints were used for the overall colour of the models. Vallejo water-based paint and Humbrol enamels were used for the detail. Oil paints were used for figure painting and weathering washes.

Pastel powders

The weathering effects on the models portrayed in this book relied heavily on the use of chalk pastels. Several colours in earth tones are handy, including raw and burnt umber, raw and burnt sienna, orange, black and white.

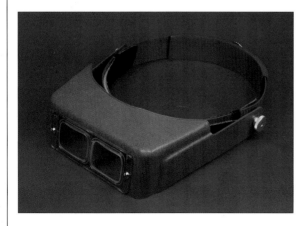

An Opti-Visor with a X3 lens came in very handy for the fine detail work. Some of the smaller etched-metal parts from Aber would have been impossible to manipulate without the use of this magnifier.

One of the essential elements in any vignette is the groundwork. Celluclay is a fine papier-mâché material that when coloured and mixed with white glue makes a base for grass, trees and other foliage.

May 1944 BMM production Hetzer

Subject:	May 1944 BMM production Hetzer
Model by:	Gary Edmundson
Skill level:	Intermediate
Basic kit:	Dragon Models Ltd. 'Early Hetzer' kit no. 6030
Tracks:	Model Kasten 'Early Hetzer' no. SK-28
Etched–metal detail:	Aber set no. 3512 'Early Hetzer' and Hetzer Fenders no. 3514
Road wheels, idlers and drive sprockets:	Fort Duquesne Miniatures Early Hetzer set FDA 104
Gun barrel:	Elefant Model Accessories no. 35.334 75mm Pak 39 L/48

An 'early' Hetzer can be regarded as one built between April and the end of June 1944. At Camp Borden in Ontario, Canada, is an example of a May production Hetzer. Captured by Canadian troops in Europe and brought back for evaluation, it sat in CFB Borden's Worthington Park for many years, and recently underwent restoration. Since this vehicle has many features of the earlier Hetzers and has been well documented, with photos in books and on the Internet, it served as the main reference for the model featured here.

In the mid-1990s Dragon models introduced their first 1/35-scale Hetzer model. DML kit number 6030 was a well-tooled early version of the Hetzer, and it serves as the base for the model. As mentioned in the introduction, the model measures out well dimensionally. The one discrepancy I did find was the length of the bottom plate, which is 2.5mm short, possibly be due to the rear plate being at too vertical an angle.

With the kit, aftermarket parts, and references ready the modeller can get started!

Since the suspension of the early Hetzers didn't compensate for the weight of the gun, the kit suspension is set so that the nose of the vehicle is 3mm lower than the tail end.

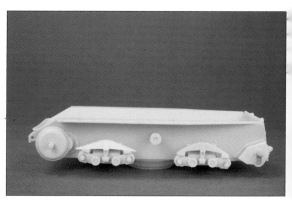

The sit of the swing arms is set after aligning the roadwheels. Care must be taken to cement these arms perpendicular to the ground.

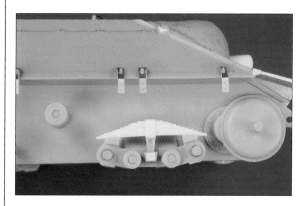

New leaf-spring assemblies were built for the front to demonstrate the flattening due to weight distribution. Note the plate at the bottom of the assembly that has 6 bolts.

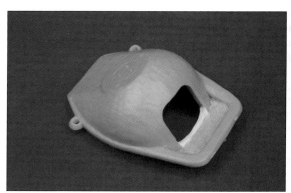

The *Kugellafette* needs to have an insert added at the bottom of the opening, and the 'chin' needs to be filled with putty.

Running gear and suspension

One of the problems with the initial Hetzer production was the forward shift in weight that the gun assembly put on the chassis. Designed for a more centred turret configuration, the hull tended to sit lower at the front than at the rear by 10cm.

To replicate this 'nose-down' look, the swing arms of the kit that hold each wheel have to be positioned so that the front of the model sits approximately 3mm lower than the rear. Because the front suspension had to bear this extra weight, the front leaf springs tended to be more flattened than the rear ones. New leaf springs were made from strips of .010in. styrene using the kit parts as a guide. They were bent into a flatter shape than the rear ones. The housing for the leaf springs has no reinforcing rib down the middle as provided on the kit parts, and this should be removed.

The bottom sections of the kit leaf-spring assemblies have two rivet heads. There was in fact a rectangular plate located there, adorned by six bolt heads. Small sections of .005in. styrene were glued in place, and small bolt heads, shaved from the underside of the kit, were positioned on them. Although not always the case, the leaf spring and mount parts can have some distinct sink marks. In this case new assemblies should be made using the method previously described.

The DML Hetzer kits all suffer from 'wobbly wheel' syndrome. The mounting posts on the swing arms are a bit too small for the hole on the back side of the

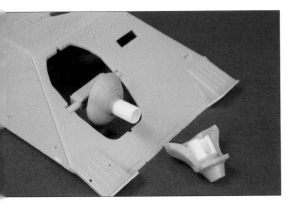

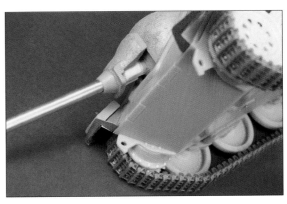

An addition was made to the lower end of the ball mount with putty, and it was positioned forward to eliminate the gap with the *Kugellafette* opening.

The gun and mantlet were slid onto the smaller tubing during construction.

wheel, and the result is a sloppy fit. Adding small pieces of adhesive lead foil onto the posts can help give the wheels a tighter fit. The swing arms themselves need careful alignment on their mounts, ensuring the roadwheels stay perpendicular to the ground.

The return roller mounts on the kit need bolt and strengthening rib detail added. Small ribs run the length of the mount at the 12.00, 4.30, and 7.30 'clock' positions. These were made with .010in. styrene card. Grant Line no. 127 bolt heads were glued into the base of the mount at the approximate 'clock' positions of 1.30, 3.00, 6.00, 9.00 and 10.30.

Small bolt heads were added to the inside edges of the final drive housings, mating up with the heads on the other side.

Road wheels

The Hetzer's road wheels were bigger than the standard Panzer 38(t), as the chassis had been developed from the 'neuer Art' version. Thirty-two bolts held a large rim and tyre onto the original size PzKpfw 38(t) wheel, giving it a larger diameter. The DML road wheels are correct in dimension, but have no bolt detail on the back face. The bolt detail on the hub of the kit wheel is also ill defined. These problems can be corrected in a couple of ways.

If the kit wheels are used, the back face of the wheel has three ejector pin marks that have to be removed with a rounded hobby knife. Inside the wheel hub, 16 Grant Line no. 127 nuts need to be added to a styrene ring. After marking the 32 locations for the inside outer rim, hex bolt heads are glued into place.

There have been some aftermarket resin Hetzer wheels produced by model companies that have done the job of detailing the backs of the road wheels, and the examples used on this model were made by Fort Duquesne Miniatures. This resin detail set also has drive sprockets and rear idlers featuring detailed inner surfaces. There are some ejector pin marks on the rear idler, as well as some sink marks on both the idler and drive sprocket parts provided in the kit that have to be filled and sanded. These are taken care of on the resin examples. Although it can be a rather expensive alternative, resin detail sets can sometimes save valuable construction time.

Tracks

The track links provided in the DML kit are nicely moulded individual pieces, but are of a later pattern than those used on the early vehicles. The early links had a single rib in the centre, and the guide horn had a thin outline on the face. The later tracks had a double rib in the centre, and the guide horn had a noticeably thicker face near the top.

The resin wheels feature interior detail, and they eliminate the poor hub detail and sink marks on the kit parts.

A new sliding cover plate for the gun sight was made from styrene. The guard over the gun sight was not centred on this vehicle, although it was on some later vehicles.

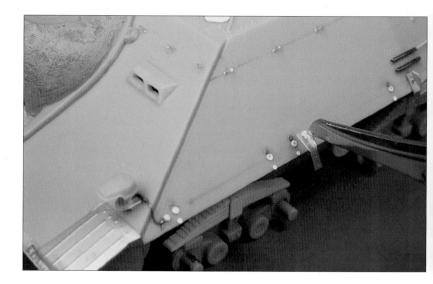

Spacers for the armoured skirt brackets were positioned on the side of the hull. The brackets were actually mounted on welded bolts, and sat proud of the surface.

The turned aluminium barrel used on this model featured the threads for a muzzle break. The barrel is made by Elefant Model Accessories, and had to be 'lathed' down on a Dremel tool to fit.

Syringe needles were cut and shaped for the spare antennae holders. Brass rod was bent and cemented into pre-drilled holes for the grab handles on the engine access doors.

Tamiya's PzKpfw IV On Vehicle Equipment Set provided the tools, and Aber's brass detail the clamps. Although tricky to assemble, the tool clamps greatly enhance the detail.

The rear tow cable was made from nylon string with ends from the Tamiya OVE set. A small wing nut was added to fasten the damper on the cooling air outlet.

Model Kasten make a set of early Hetzer tracks and set SK-28 was used here. It takes approximately four hours of careful work to make two runs of 96 links. Assembly consists of clipping each of the links off their sprue, assembling ten at a time onto the jig provided, and placing the small pin into the holes to join them. The tiny pins were liberally coated in Testor's liquid cement before 'wiggling' them into place to form a secure bond. A small amount of clean-up is required with a sharp no. 11 X-acto blade.

Gun, mantlet and *Kugellafette*

The kit part for the large cast-metal housing for the gun assembly, or *Kugellafette*, has a deep gaping chin that needed to be filled with putty. Missing from this kit (but included in the later releases) is a lower portion of the assembly that frames the gun opening. This gap was filled with a piece of styrene. The large protruding lugs near the top of the casting also needed a level of putty added to the centres.

The ball mount for the gun was modified to cover the opening closely, since there is too much of a gap near the bottom. Epoxy putty was added to the part and shaped with a file and sandpaper. The part was also spun on a Dremel tool and touched with course sandpaper to give it the fine lines of a 'machined' look.

The mantlet mount on the gun was fashioned using $^9/_{32}$in. diameter styrene tubing. The piece was filed down and grooved on the bottom before gluing into the mantlet. A section of $^7/_{32}$in. tubing was then glued to the ball mount. Weld marks at the joint were added with epoxy putty, and the mantlet mount was then slid into position onto the smaller diameter tubing.

The gun barrel was replaced with a more accurate turned-aluminium product that features a threaded end. As some Hetzers had the muzzle breaks of the 7.5cm guns removed, the bare threads were left exposed.

An improvement can be made to the cast-metal texture of both the mantlet and *Kugellafette* by scraping off the kit's bumpy surface with a hobby blade and then adding Tamiya putty to the parts. The putty should be spread in an even layer, and then textured with an old toothbrush.

Etched brass

The advent of brass detail sets has provided the modeller with opportunities to add a wealth of accuracy to their models. Some of the more standard parts that etched brass is most helpful with are the tarpaulin attachment loops, tool brackets and engine air outlet screen.

Model Kasten's SK-28 track was added to the kit. The guide horns had to be shortened by 1mm where they met the drive sprocket.

The *Kugellafette* and mantlet received a cast-metal texture by applying a thin layer of Tamiya lacquer-based putty and texturing it with an old toothbrush.

Aber produced the etched-brass mudguards for the kit, and the brackets were soldered together for strength.

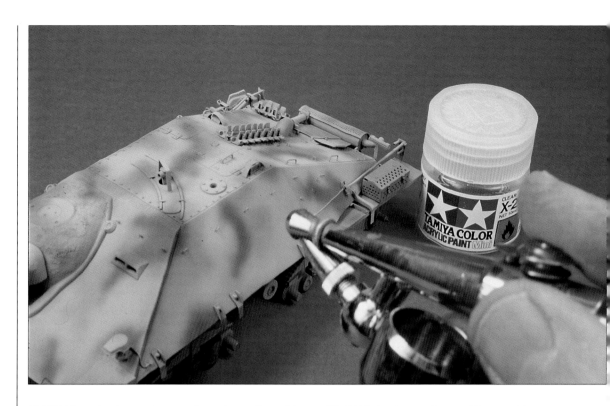

ABOVE After airbrushing on the camouflage scheme, the model was prepared for decals by spraying an area with clear gloss.

BELOW Only white numbers could be found the correct size, so the inside was painted on with Vallejo Black.

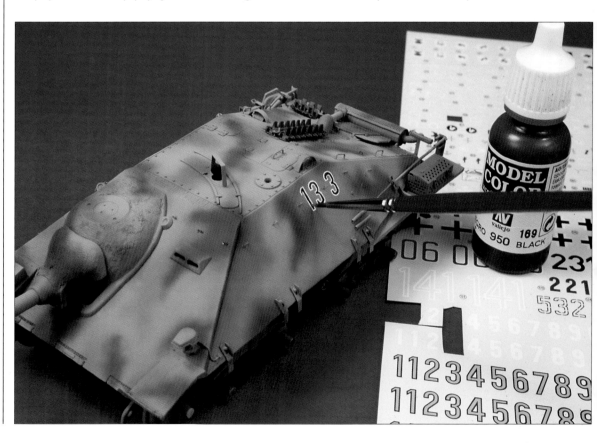

Before attaching the side skirts, the finished tracks were put in place, and the tension adjusted with the idler's moveable axle.

The Aber set for the early Hetzer was used here, as was the mudguard set. Working with brass allows the small lip to be shown on the front mudguard, just below the bracket. The mudguards and brackets were soldered together for strength before attaching them to the model with cyano glue.

Hull detail – rear plate

The rear plate was a solid piece from left to right, and the joints on the kit need to be filled and sanded flat accordingly. Weld marks can be made on the edges by dragging an X-acto blade sideways down the corners.

The towing pintles of the vehicle were extensions of the hull side plates. Since the plates were 20mm thick, the kit parts need to be thinned down or rebuilt with .015in. styrene. The rear towing pintles need to be positioned higher than the kit instructions illustrate, with the top sitting 3mm below the rearmost mudguardbracket.

The tow bar, a prominent feature on the early vehicles, had an internal support that had four bolts on each of the hull sides by the rear plate. Bolt heads made from styrene hex rod were cut and positioned on the left and right hull sides, just ahead of where the tow bar joins the rear plate.

Moulding restrictions result in the external starter mounts being tapered, so these should be replaced with styrene rod. To create the knob effect on the end, the rods were spun in a Dremel tool, and 'lathed' into shape with a no. 11 blade.

The towing cables for the Hetzer were held in place with three 'J'-shaped pieces of flat metal that had leather straps attached to them. Aber's brass detail set was used for these, along with a cable made from fine nylon string and a couple of cable ends from Tamiya's Pz. IV Vehicle Equipment accessory set.

Tightening a clamp on the adjustment screw locked the rear idler position. The Aber brass part is one dimensional, and the clamp assembly had to be built with small pieces of styrene set at an angle toward the top of the vehicle.

Hull detail – upper hull

The tarpaulin fasteners on the hull side of the early vehicle were lower then those on the DML kit. After removing the kit's impressions, a pencil line was drawn 5.5mm from the top edge and etched-brass ones were added.

The hatch handles were swapped with ones fashioned from .015in. brass rod. The kit's locating holes were first drilled out and plugged with styrene rod, then appropriately sized holes were drilled to accept the replacements.

The screw head detail on the crew hatches is overstated in the kit, so the depressions were filled with Tamiya's lacquer-based putty. Royal Model's no. 34 etched-brass screw heads were used here as they sit closer to the surface of the hatch.

Small strips of styrene were glued to the side-skirt brackets, and the skirts themselves positioned using liquid cement. They were cemented securely with cyano glue when correctly aligned.

The nose-down profile of the vehicle is evident.

The driver's visor had the openings cut out with a drill bit, then trimmed with a sharp no. 11 X-acto blade.

The rear mudguards of the Hetzer sloped downward to the outside, and the brass examples were bent to reflect this.

Brass screw heads by Royal Model were used on the crew hatches. A pin that moved the sliding plate was added just to the right of the gun-sight guard.

The two tool clamps on the jack were arranged in opposite directions on this vehicle. Some had them going the same direction. The vehicle antenna is from DML's German Antennae Set.

The vehicle was washed with thinner and raw umber oil paints. The wash was thicker around the roadwheel hubs, which tended to show grease stains with use.

Although the etched-metal detail for the remote machine gun dresses it up nicely, the actuating wire and spring return on the trigger need to be added with thin copper wire.

There are a couple of significant pin-ejector marks on the cover for the gun sight hole in the roof. Either careful sanding or construction of a new part from styrene should fix that problem. The cover needs to have four small retainers added to the front and rear curved guides.

After adding the Aber details to the Notek lamp above the left front fender, a conduit for the electrical lead was added using very thin solder wire. This wire is actually sold in fishing supply shops, and used to tie flies. The openings for the armoured periscope cover were drilled out.

On the rear left side of the vehicle are two bolt heads with a small round disc in the middle. This was the port for the command vehicle's additional antenna. The disc needs to be moved just slightly to the rear of its current position.

The spare antenna mounts consist of a rear socket with four locations, two small lengths of tubing at the front, and a fastener in the middle. The tubing was made by carefully cutting off the end of a syringe needle and bending it to fit the contour of the vehicle. A spare antenna was taken from the DML German Tank Antennae set (kit no. 3819), and placed in position. Both the Aber and the DML kit parts for the rear mount have the locations positioned incorrectly; a new one should be made from styrene (see the chapters on the late and sIG33 versions). The earlier vehicles positioned this mount at the very rear of the left fender.

The skirt armour brackets were actually mounted on large bolts welded to the hull. As a result the brackets themselves sat proud of the hull after being fastened in place. After filling in the kit's mounting depressions, a line was drawn 2.5mm from the bottom edge of the hull and .012in. styrene discs were added as mounting washers. The brackets were centred slightly lower than the locating holes on the kit. A smaller second disc was glued just below this for stability. After positioning the bracket in place, Grant Line no. 127 nuts were glued at the top of the slots to secure them.

The tool brackets and clasps used on the models came from the Aber line of etched-metal details and are of the 'workable' type. Care, patience and a sharp eye are needed for assembly, but the resulting detail is worth the effort. The tool clamps on the jack, stowed on the rear right fender, are facing opposite directions. Some later vehicles, such as the Hetzer at the Tank Museum, Bovington, UK, had hem positioned facing the same way. It is a detail to note when modelling a particular vehicle.

The jack block located on the front right mudguard was made of laminated wood held together with three metal bands all fastened down with a large wing nut. The banding was flush to the surface of the jack face, and the wood actually stuck proud of the metal on the corners. The kit's block was improved by sanding down the surface slightly, and rounding off the corners of the three bands. The edge of the metal was scribed onto the sides of the block with a sharp no. 11 blade.

Notes on painting and markings

The vehicle was painted to match the reference colour plate A2 in Osprey's New Vanguard 36. The vehicle was built in May 1944 at the BMM factory in Prague, and features a colour scheme of overall Dunkelgelb RAL 7028 with sprayed-on patches of Olivgrün RAL 6003 and Rotbraun RAL 8017.

The model was primed by airbrushing on dark-brown Floquil lacquer, followed by at least 48 hours of setting time. A mixture of Tamiya XF-59 Desert Yellow and XF-60 Dark Yellow was misted on, allowing the shadow effect of the primer to show through. Thinned Tamiya Red brown, followed by Model Master Panzer Olivgrün was airbrushed on to form the camouflage pattern.

The surface of the model was prepared by airbrushing the area with acrylic gloss and allowing it to dry thoroughly before sliding the decals into position. Solvaset was brushed on to help them soften and meld to the hull. To replicate the correct size, the vehicle's white tactical numbers were cut from one of Tamiya's accessory decal sheets, then had a black center painted by hand with Vallejo paint.

After weathering the entire surface with a light spray of acrylic dust colour, the model received a wash of oil paints in mineral spirit. To add character and detail to the surface, scuffs and scrapes to the paint surface were added in a random pattern using a fine-tipped 000 brush.

A mixture of Humbrol silver enamel and raw umber oil paint was drybrushed to give a worn metallic look to the end of the barrel, drive sprocket teeth and areas of wear from the crew.

ABOVE A matt coat of Testor's Model Master Flat Lacquer was used to seal the areas where the decals were applied.

BELOW The Hetzer sits outside its place of manufacture – the BMM factory in Prague.

May 1945 Skoda production Hetzer

Subject:	*May 1945 Skoda production Hetzer*
Model by:	*Gary Edmundson*
Skill level:	*Advanced*
Basic kit:	*Dragon Models Ltd. 'Jagdpanzer/Flammpanzer 38 Mid Production' kit no. 6037*
Tracks:	*Model Kasten 'Late Hetzer' no. SK-29*
Etched–metal detail:	*Aber set no. 3513 'Late Hetzer' and Hetzer Fenders no. 3514*
Gun barrel:	*CMK Hotbarrels no. HB036*
Resin Interior Detail:	*Verlinden Productions Hetzer Interior no. 1692, and Hetzer Engine and Compartment no. 1097*

The later version of the Hetzer modelled here was built by the Skoda Works in Pilsen, Czechoslovakia, during the last month of the war, and had the serial number Fgst.nr. 323814. It was captured by US forces, and sent to the United States for evaluation at the Aberdeen Proving Ground. This example of the Hetzer features many of the modifications that were implemented during the development of the vehicle.

One of the first steps in adding a complete interior to this vehicle is to determine what aftermarket kit parts are available, and to what extent the interior will be seen. The model shown in this section has both a detailed engine and fighting compartment. A removable roof was fitted so that the detail can be exposed. As a basis for this work, I used the Verlinden Productions Hetzer Interior and Hetzer Engine and Compartment with the DML kit no. 6037

Lower hull interior detail – firewall

The interior and engine compartment detail sets both provide a rear firewall. To feature both compartments, a new firewall needs to be built from .015in. styrene sheet. A template was made from paper, and fiddled with until the

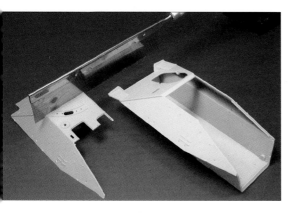

In order to expose the interior detail, the roof was made to be removable. A new one was taken from a spare upper hull left over from a conversion project. Careful trimming was important for an exact fit.

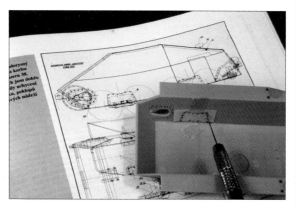

The locations for the internal bolt patterns of the drive housings and suspension supports were marked with a needle after tracing a technical drawing.

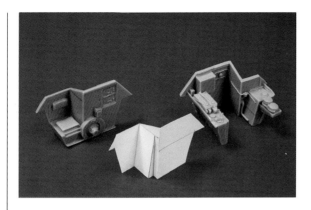

Since the resin detail sets come with a one-sided bulkhead, or firewall, one was constructed from styrene by first making a paper form that could be modified easily for a correct fit. The fillet by the commander's seat position was necessary for the fit of the engine components.

The completed firewall, with the resin drive housing from the VP set. Detail was added with solder wire, lead foil and styrene strip. The scissors scope mount to the right of the commander's seat was made with various sizes of styrene rod and stretched sprue.

New leaf-spring assemblies were made to show the increased dimension of the front one in the later vehicles. The spring elements were increased in size from 7 to 9mm, so a corresponding change was made to the kit.

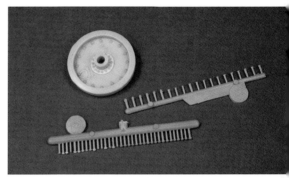

Interior detail was added to the kit's road wheels. After filling the injection moulding marks, a ring of 16 bolt heads was added to the hub. Grant Line no. 154 rivet heads were added to where the rim attached.

correct dimensions were attained. The dimensions of the hatches on the engine deck help determine where the bulkhead needs to be positioned, and test-fitting confirms the location. Because the engine was tilted to the left at 15 degrees from the vertical, the left wall of the commander's position was angled to accommodate this.

A 12.5mm square box 5mm deep was made for the radios, and cemented to the rear once an appropriate opening to the firewall had been made. The two radio components (Fu 5) were the 10 W.S.c transmitter and a Uk.E.e receiver. These were scratch-built, cast in resin and given mounts standard to installations in most German AFVs of World War II. The power supplies for each component were mounted just below the radio box and these were made from laminated pieces of .040in. and .020in. styrene to get the correct thickness. The radios were wired using thin solder wire. Wiring between the radios and the intercom box was completed at a later stage in construction once the upper and lower hull halves were joined.

The housing for the motor's final drive was removed from the resin firewall, and positioned so that the drive shaft was centred with the transmission. Clipped to the top of this housing was a multi-purpose wrench that was made from etched-brass toolbox details.

Three of the ammunition stowage racks, made from scraps of styrene and sized to fit VP resin 75mm ammo. Use of a punch and die set helped in the construction of these assemblies.

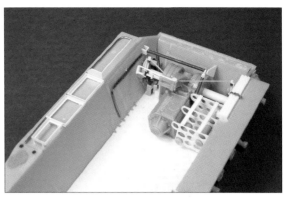

The transmission area was modified to include steering components and the clutch linkage. The racks on the left sponson held equipment such as extra radios (for the command tanks) or ammunition.

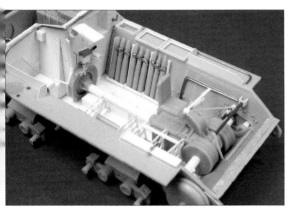

The nine-round ready-rack was located behind the driver, and was detailed with lead straps and etched-metal buckles. Located at the top of the firewall and reaching forward is the fume extractor ducting, fashioned from laminated pieces of .080in. and .040in. styrene.

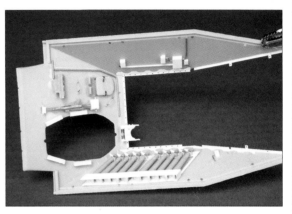

Components of the upper hull had to be test-fitted at each stage to ensure there would be no interference with the gun breech. A scalloped strip was added to the perimeter of the opening, made by snipping a styrene strip with a hole-punch.

The commander's position was located on the lower portion of the right fuel tank. The seat cushion was positioned on a stowage box, with a Czechoslovakian-style fire extinguisher in the right-hand corner. The wall behind the commander was detailed using .005in. styrene sheet with small rivet heads, outlining the upper section of the fuel tank.

Lower hull interior detail – transmission and final drive

To detail the kit where the final drive shafts exit the hull, the openings at the front were cut out following a detailed drawing in the MBI book on the Hetzer. Internal bolt detail was added around the circumference for the exterior drive housings, and also where the mounts for the roadwheel suspension assemblies were attached.

Each final drive shaft has a steering component mounted where it leaves the hull. These components were modelled from strip and rod, and then cemented into position on the shafts. The left one in front of the driver was located behind the shaft, and the right one was ahead of the shaft. The tops of the

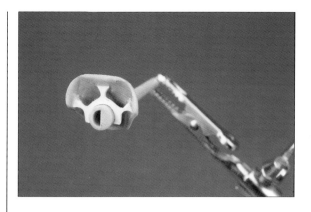

The inside of the mantlet had a support that made a three-point contact. After constructing the support from .040in. sheet, the mantlet had to be 'beefed up' with epoxy putty to accept it.

Putty was added to the sunken chin of the *Kugellafette*, and the stops for the gun cemented into place.

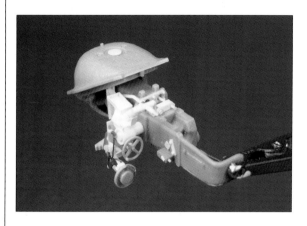

The gun's breech assembly, as supplied in the VP interior detail set, needs to be modified from a StuK 40 to a Pak 39/L48 wartime example. Styrene tube, and odds and ends from the scrap box helped complete the job.

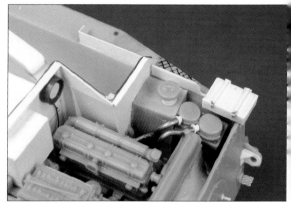

The VP engine and components were adapted to the new firewall. The VP set includes the later type of air filters, located behind the fuel tank with air lines made from solder running to the carburetor. I scratchbuilt the earlier style of air filter, seen sitting on the corner at the back of the vehicle, to show the difference. The earlier example would have been located on top of the fuel tank

assemblies were attached to the steering lever hub with long rods. The driver's steering levers were made from thin styrene strips to get the right length.

The clutch pedal linkage followed a large horizontal bar supported just in front of the driver. The bar led the linkage to the right side of the transmission. A small length of copper wire was bent from the clutch pedal up to a styrene rod, and linkage created from a box of styrene bits and pieces.

Lower hull interior detail – ammunition stowage

Although this model is based on the Aberdeen Proving Ground vehicle, ammunition stowage was modelled to show a more typical earlier example. Forty-one rounds of both high-explosive and armour-piercing rounds were stowed. Later modifications added five more rounds. There was a rack of nine rounds to the immediate left of the gunner's and loader's seats. To the right of the transmission was a metal 'wine rack' holding 10 rounds, and right behind that was a collapsible rack containing another 12. Two angled racks were bolted on the upper right armour plate above the sponson, and these stored ten rounds.

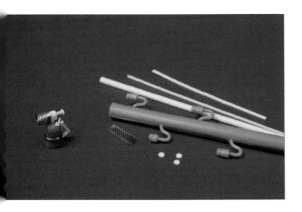

The vehicle's blowtorch was constructed from the various bits and pieces shown.

The resin Praga AC engine was painted with Vallejo and Humbrol paints, and weathered with pastel chalks.

A suitable colour for the red primer was determined using a piece of *zimmerit* that still had traces of the colour (on the right hand edge).

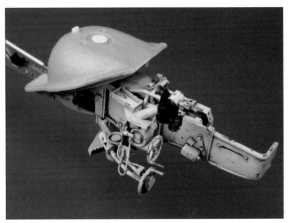

The completed breech assembly, weathered with a wash of thinned raw umber oil paint. Above the traverse and elevation controls is the support for the gun sight.

The racks were modelled around the Verlinden set of 75mm ammunition using a punch and die set, and various thicknesses of styrene sheet. The resin shells have to be placed fairly close together, since the hull interior suffers from lack of 'scale' space due to the thickness of the wall of the kit. Test-fitting of the racks is very important to ensure that there is no interference with the other interior components. Paper forms were tacked into place on the model's interior as a guide for the size and shape of the eventual rack.

Lower hull interior detail – miscellaneous

The area above the sponsons on the left-hand side had mounting frames for radios and/or other equipment. Ahead of those, adjacent to the driver, was a stowage bin. A similar stowage bin was located to the commander's right side, just behind the angled ammo racks. At the front of the right sponson sat a stowage area for the gun cleaning rods. All of these details were constructed from styrene rod and strip.

The seats for the loader and gunner were built with scrap plastic, and enhanced with seat cushions made from epoxy putty. The cushions were upholstered with two buttons, and were fastened to the metal stanchions by four canvas straps. Two toolboxes were made from laminated plastic (to make them thick enough). They were located on the floor below the drive shaft.

The upper hull's interior after most of the components were fitted. The interior was finished in an ivory colour, sprayed over a dark-brown primer.

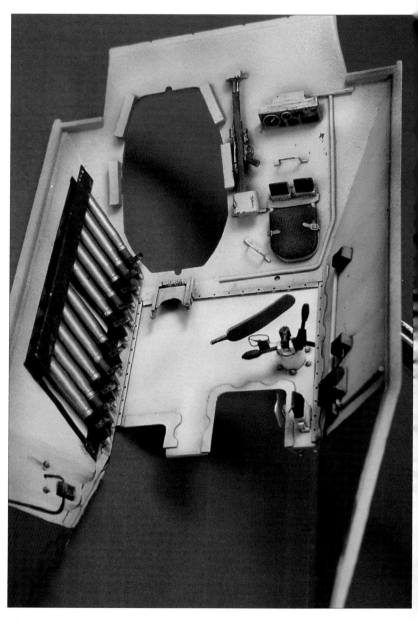

Upper hull interior detail

Since this model was to have a fully detailed fighting compartment, the roof plate was modelled to lift off for viewing. One option was to scratch-build one with styrene sheet. Since a conversion kit was used to make the Bergepanzer in a later chapter, there was a spare roof available and this was used here. Angle support was made using .010in. styrene, added around the perimeter of the roof at the appropriate height on the hull walls once the boltholes had been drilled. Scalloped styrene strip, representing the downward leg of the connection angle for the roof plate, was placed against the hull walls just below the roof flange. The roof plate was thinned down by carefully sanding it. Stoppers for the hatches were cut and added, and the slot for the main gun sight carved out.

A firing station for the remote machine gun was fabricated from scrap plastic, and added to the inside of the roof plate with some surrounding bolt detail. The left handle was placed in the 'swung down' position to clear the wall as it rotated.

The hatch interior detail was mostly provided by the Aber 'Late Hetzer' brass detail set. One of the simple locking handles for the commander's side was made with lead wire. The elaborate latch on the loader's hatch was moved from the left side on the early vehicles to the right on the later ones.

Periscopes made from the parts box were given small fasteners on either side, and glued into position on the loader and commander's hatches. Some later Hetzers also had a head pad on the commander's hatch, but the Aberdeen example shows no evidence of this.

After adding the driver's periscopes, a head pad made from epoxy putty was glued onto a solder wire support. Closer examination of the museum example shows this support to be off-centre to the left. To the right of the driver was mounted the StG 44 assault rifle. A Tamiya gun was trimmed front and back, and styrene blocks added to represent the supports.

Junction boxes and the intercom box were linked with fine solder wire. Conduits for the other electrical hook-ups were handled the same way. The locations for the intercom plug-ins varied throughout the production of the vehicle.

The gun travel-lock hung from the top of the glacis, just forward of the roof plate. This spring-loaded device sat pointing straight back when not in use, and was pulled down and locked in place between engagements. The example modelled here is of a later type, the early ones only had a metal tube frame. Plastic scraps and a spring made from thin copper wire were used to fashion the lock on this model.

Beneath the roof was the control for the remote machine gun. An interior light and conduit were located just behind it.

Engine compartment

To show off the engine, the hatches on both sides were opened up. The Verlinden engine detail set for the Hetzer does supply hatches, but only for the early version of the vehicle. The later vehicles had access hatches for coolant and oil at the rear of the vehicle. The very late-war examples (including the Aberdeen example) had the coolant access welded shut, and the right hand engine hatch extended to the rear plate to access the later-style air filters. It is the late-style filters that are supplied in the Verlinden detail set. Because of the location of these filters, the shovel, sledgehammer and blowtorch had to be moved from their location by the rear plate in the engine compartment.

To model the required engine hatch configuration, the kit part had to be sanded down and the hatches carefully separated with a sharp no. 11 blade.

The metallic wear and tear to the engine compartment was added with a silver pencil. To the right of the starboard fuel tank is the mesh screen for one of the air intakes. The other would have been on the left side, hidden by the battery on the port fuel tank.

The completed fighting compartment prior to the assembly of the two halves of the hull. The wiring for the radio was hooked up to the intercom amplifier after this was done.

The floor and engine compartment were brush-painted with a mixture of Vallejo paints representing red primer. The individual 75mm rounds were black for armour piercing and green for high explosive, with Testor's gold enamel for the brass cases.

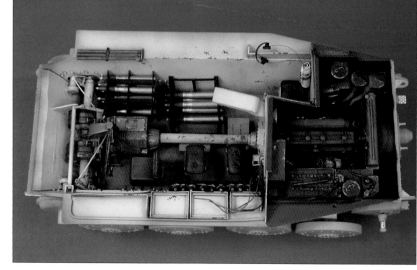

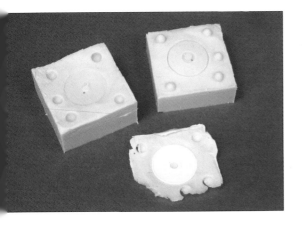

The kit's idler wheel had the holes filled with styrene, and castings were made from RTV rubber moulds and resin.

Holes were drilled in the resin discs, and the idlers were completed using the kit parts.

The left and right fuel tanks of the engine compartment were removed from the resin firewall, and cemented to the scratch-built one ensuring the fit of the motor and radiator. Since the fit was tight, air tubes leading from the air filters to each carburettor were bent from solder wire rather than trying to get the straight resin pieces to line up. The fuel filler cap was raised on the right tank with styrene rod.

Using some scraps from the parts box, a blowtorch was constructed and mounted on the firewall. The torch was used to heat the engine coolant for cold weather starts, and was attached to a receptacle at the lower right corner of the rear plate when used.

Lower hull and suspension

One of the changes made from the early Hetzers was the beefing up of the front suspension, allowing the vehicle to sit level to the ground. As a result of the changes the front leaf springs consisted of 16 9mm-thick elements in a 19.5 x 10cm housing. The rear leaf spring retained 16 7mm-thick elements in a 15 x 10cm housing. Both later front and rear housings had a reinforcement strip down the middle. The assemblies were modelled using styrene strip that was cut to match the width of the kit parts. The housing supports had a lightening hole not visible from the front, and the kit's recesses need to be filled with putty.

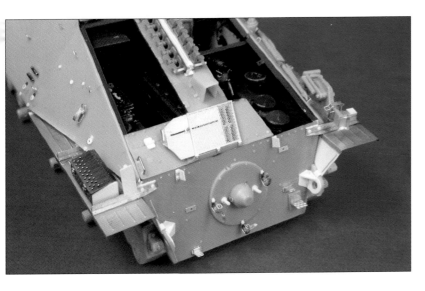

The towing pintles were strengthened with welded plates, and sat lower on the rear plate than those on the earlier vehicle.

The metal box that held the tow hooks was a hybrid kind with solid sides and a perforated front and top. Many late Hetzers featured completely solid ones. The base for the antenna mount in the kit and the Aber detail set has the mounting posts incorrectly positioned, so a new one was made from styrene.

With the change to the later style air filters, the shovel and sledge hammer moved from being stowed inside the engine compartment to the right side of the hull. Parts from Tamiya's PzKpfw IV OVE set were used here.

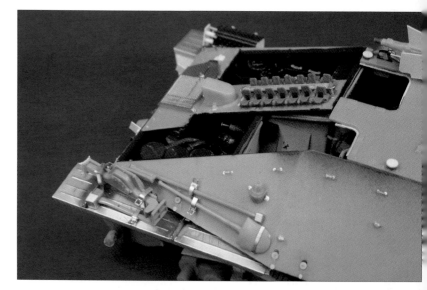

Shields for the remote MG 34 were made from styrene sheet. The left side had a couple of notches on the upper edge used to mount a bag of ammunition.

Model Kasten's SK-29 Late Hetzer track links and their drive sprockets from set A-9 complement the model.

The Czech company CMK produces aluminium gun barrels in 1/35 scale, featured here. For the towing pintle reinforcements, Aber's brass parts were used as a guide to make styrene replacements of a more realistic thickness.

Fillets were added to the inside of the rear mudguards. The tow cable supports and straps are Aber's intricate brass details.

Masks for the camouflage scheme were first sketched onto scrap kit pieces, then cut out of low-tack masking tape with a sharp no. 11 blade on a sheet of glass.

The model was first given a Dunkelgelb base and masks were applied. This was repeated with red primer, before Olivgrün was sprayed on.

The towing pintles at the rear of the vehicle were located lower down than the ones on the early Hetzer, and were reinforced with metal plates. The reinforced plate was also added to the front towing pintles. Although it's provided in the brass detail sets, this feature is best replicated with .010in. styrene.

Running gear

Later vehicles featured a larger wheel disc, and therefore had narrower tyre rims. The rims were riveted as opposed to the earlier bolted style, so to detail the inside of the wheels, Grant Line rivet heads were used.

At least seven variants of the rear idler were used throughout the development of the Hetzer, the Aberdeen example has the latest one. A resin casting of the kit's six-hole idler was made after filling the holes with thin styrene to make a master. The resulting blank castings were drilled with the appropriate holes, and adapted to the kit parts.

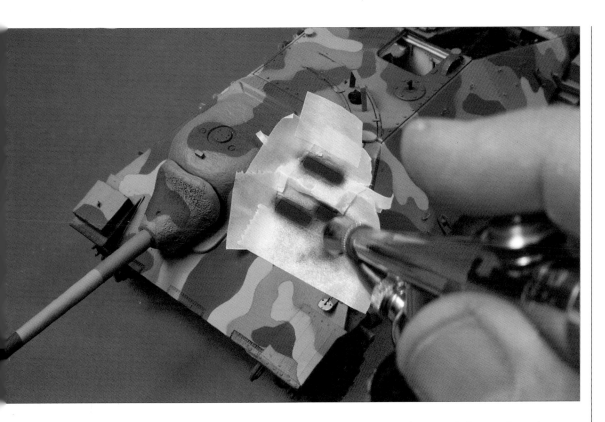

ABOVE Black bars were painted near the driver's visor to fool enemy gunners as to its location. Thin rectangles were masked off and Tamiya Black was sprayed on.

BELOW With all the masks removed, the camouflage scheme received touch-ups with a brush on areas where the tape had not sat down in corners and around details.

ABOVE The completed model, with all the side skirts and access hatches attached.

BELOW The streaked effect on the sides of the model was achieved by dragging small spots of raw umber oil paint down using a brush moistened with thinner.

ABOVE The engine hatch on the right side was enlarged to gain access to the air filters. The small coolant hatch was welded closed, and the rear panel cut and welded to the engine hatch itself.

BELOW The model received a dusting of thinned Tamiya acrylic paint made up of an earth-coloured mix. It was concentrated on the lower regions, but sprayed everywhere to tone down the vivid camouflage scheme

Oil paint washes were used around all of the cracks and crevices of the model using Winsor & Newton Black, Raw Umber and Burnt Sienna.

Tracks

A new style of tracks was introduced during the summer of 1944, with vehicles sometimes showing a mixture of both new and old styles. The later tracks had a thicker face at the top of the guide horn, and a second rib in the center of the tread. I have not seen any photos of wartime vehicles with the notches in the tread, as shown on some G-13 examples. Model Kasten's SK- 29 Late Hetzer tracks were used on this model.

Gun, mantlet and *Kugellafette*

Although it is an accurate rendition of the Aberdeen vehicle's main weapon, the kit gun barrel was replaced with one from CMK Hotbarrels, and set in the mantlet to have a length of 46.5mm. A support for the mantlet to fit around the barrel was made from .020in. styrene, and test-fitted several times before it was cemented in place. The inside of the mantlet needs to be thickened with epoxy putty. The procedure for modifying the *Kugellafette* and ball mount on the early Hetzer was repeated on this model, with the addition of welded-on stops for the gun elevation and traverse limits.

Upper hull exterior detail

The shroud for the exhaust lined up parallel to vehicle's centreline, not at the more common angle. DML's kit provides the wider vertically oriented exhaust with flame arrester, or *Flamm-Vernichter*, so the horizontally mounted silencer (without the perforated shroud) needed for this example had to be scrounged from another kit.

Details requiring a worn-metal look were highlighted with a soft graphite pencil.

The silencer received a heavy coating of pastel chalks, as did the inside of the engine hatches. A graphite pencil was rubbed onto the spare track links to accent the corners.

The visor over the driver's periscopes had the rain lip removed. Many vehicles did not feature this lip. Three styrene tube '*pilzen*' were added in the appropriate locations on the roof plate. These allowed the vehicle to have a hoist mounted for maintenance.

The shields for the remote machine gun were made from .010in. styrene with the left one featuring two small notches along the top. The notches allowed the mounting an ammunition bag as an alternative to the 50-round drums carried.

The hinges on all access doors and hatches were welded on the later vehicles, and so the kit's bolts were removed.

Notes on painting and markings

The original colour scheme applied at the Skoda factory featured on this vehicle was a standard pattern seen in numerous period photographs. Although not every vehicle was identical, the patches of hard-edged colour followed a similar pattern.

With a wealth of detail built into the model, a removable roof plate was an important element in the build of the late Hetzer.

The decision on what colour to paint this model was difficult, with some references contradicting each other. I had three black and white photos of the original camouflage scheme from two reference books, including Osprey's New Vanguard 36. A colour picture of the Aberdeen vehicle taken shortly after the war appears in the book *German Tanks Of World War II In Colour* by Motorbooks International, and it was this that determined the model's eventual scheme.

The interior of the vehicle was first sprayed with a dark-brown primer followed by a light misting of Vallejo's Ivory White. The floor of the fighting compartment and the vehicle's engine bay were brush-painted a red primer colour made up of Vallejo water based colours. After painting in all of the details the entire interior was weathered with an oil paint/thinner mixture, then given a 'lived in' look with the application of subtle paint chipping.

After priming the exterior of the model with Floquil dark brown, a base coat of dark-yellow acrylic was airbrushed on. The model was masked using patches of painter's low-tack masking tape that were cut out on a pane of glass with a sharp hobby knife. A coat of red primer followed, with masking patches again being applied after the surface had thoroughly dried. A final coat of Model Master acrylic Panzer Olivgrün was airbrushed on, and all of the masking then removed.

A very dilute acrylic dirt colour was sprayed onto the model, concentrating on the lower regions. When dry, oil paint thinned with mineral spirits was applied to all surfaces, paying particular attention to the wheel hubs and panel lines. The oil paint was dragged down the side plates of the hull to emulate the dirt and rain streaks accumulated in field service. Scrapes to the paint finish were simulated by mixing a dark grey Vallejo paint, and randomly adding it with a fine 000 brush. A mixture of Hudson & Allen mud and various pastel chalks were mixed with water and added in a stippling fashion to the lower areas of the hull and running gear with an old paintbrush.

15cm Schweres Infanteriegeschütz 33/2 (Sf) auf Jagdpanzer 38(t) Hetzer

Subject:	*15cm Schweres Infanteriegeschütz 33/2 (Sf) auf Jagdpanzer 38(t) Hetzer*
Model by:	*Gary Edmundson*
Skill level:	*Master*
Basic kit:	*Dragon Models Ltd. 'Early Hetzer' kit no. 6030*
Resin conversion kit:	*New Connection Models SIG 33 on Hetzer, heavy infantry gun, no. 35002*
Tracks:	*Model Kasten 'Early Hetzer' no. SK-28*
Etched–metal detail:	*Aber set no. 3512 'Early Hetzer' and Hetzer Fenders no. 3514*
Road wheels, idlers and drive sprockets:	*Fort Duquesne Miniatures Early Hetzer set no. FDA 104*

Since the need for a self-propelled 15cm gun continued after production of the PzKpfw 38(t) Ausf. M had ceased, the Germans decided to mount the sIG 33/2 gun on the Jagdpanzer 38(t) chassis. In September 1944 a prototype of this vehicle was built at the BMM factory on Hetzer chassis number 321079 (produced in May). German sources say that 30 of these vehicles were built at the Alkett factory in Germany. Completed between the months of December 1944 and February 1945, six were built from modified Jagdpanzer vehicles, and the rest were new builds. This model represents the prototype vehicle.

Resin conversion kits

Recent years have brought the modeller numerous modification and detail sets to enhance or create different versions of existing kits. Soon after a kit is produced, modellers who want to take their model to a higher level of detail and authenticity eagerly await release of these aftermarket sets.

Several conversion sets are available to modify the Dragon (or Italeri) Hetzer models into the numerous variants seen during and after World War II. The kit used in this instance was made by New Connection of Germany, and is used in conjunction with the Dragon kit no. 6030 'Early Hetzer'. For the purposes of this feature, the entire conversion kit was not used.

Preliminary research

After reviewing the parts of the New Connections kit, careful scrutiny should be made of the vehicle the modeller wants to replicate, and how the kit measures up. The reference photos of this vehicle show it to be built on an early chassis, but the kit provides a later engine deck, which needs to be changed. Since the raised structure on my resin kit was damaged, and the modifications to the DML styrene hull were simple, I decided to use the styrene hull and scratch-build the raised superstructure. As a general point it is much easier to work with styrene parts than resin ones.

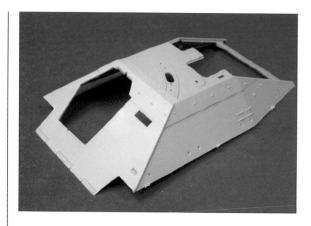

To modify the hull, the opening for the kit's *Kugellafette* was cut to an accommodating shape to accept a styrene insert.

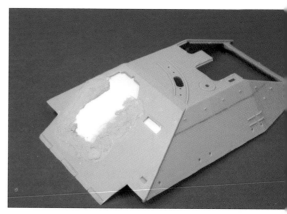

After adding a .020in. insert behind the front glacis, a .040in. fillet was cut to fit the opening, and the gaps filled with putty.

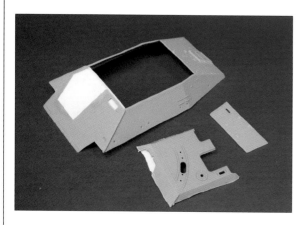

The glacis was sanded smooth, and a horizontal guideline drawn that aligned with the rear of the commander's hatch. The roof plate and engine deck hatches were cut following the pencil line, leaving enough extra to carefully sand smooth and level.

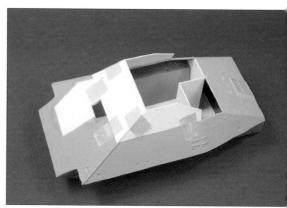

Following photo reference, technical drawings and the New Connections hull as a guide, armoured walls were cut from .015in. styrene sheet and test-fitted to the hull with tape. Styrene was also cut to form the rear firewall.

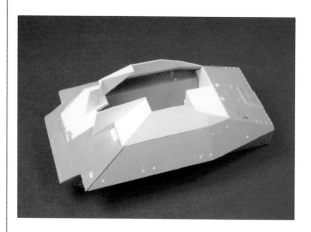

Once the basic shape of the hull was established, the rest of the upper hull's additional armour plates could be cut and cemented into position.

Zimm-It-Rite epoxy putty from R&J Enterprises was used to make some of the weld beads. The beads were textured with a toothpick after they were placed on the joint, and then trimmed with the length of a no. 11 hobby knife.

Stretched sprue, softened with liquid cement, was also used to simulate the weld beads on the model.

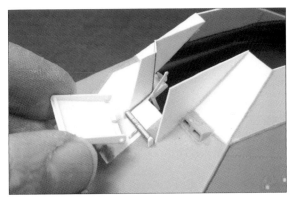

The armour plate protecting the front of the gun was under the tension of a large spring, shown here made from thin electrical wire.

The firewall, featuring the earlier-style heater outlet adjacent to the two dynamotors, which supplied power to the radios.

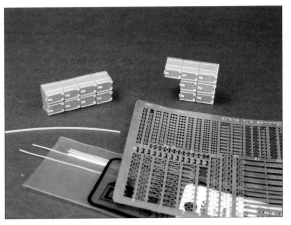

The ammunition charge boxes from the Alan Grille M kit were enhanced with brass detail from Aber, and strip and rod styrene.

Lower hull and running gear

The chassis on which this example was built featured the earlier style of road-wheels, idler and rear plate. The resin wheels from Fort Duquesne's early Hetzer set were used as per the previous chapter. The leaf-spring assemblies were an unusual hybrid on this example. The front assemblies were beefed up to include the thicker elements, but lacked the prominent reinforcing rib on the housing. The rear assembly had the reinforcing rib, but both front and rear assemblies featured the visible cavity below the leaf-spring housing.

Upper hull and additional armour

Filling the opening for the Hetzer's *Kugellafette* in the upper hull was the first step in modifying the kit. The hole was enlarged to a more receptive shape allowing a section of styrene card to be glued in place, filled with putty and sanded smooth. The putty and sanding was repeated until the glacis plate was acceptably smooth and unblemished. To increase the front glacis plate to the correct thickness, .020in. styrene sheet was cut to fit and added to the inside. A horizontal line was drawn on the upper hull of the DML Hetzer at a point intersecting the rear of the commander's hatch. Using the line as a guide, the roof plate was removed and the resulting opening sanded down level.

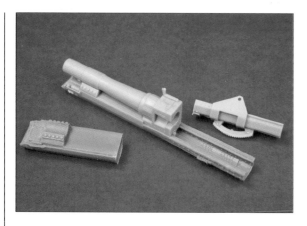

The Alan gun was adapted to The New Connection cradle, taking the best of both kits to make an accurate one.

The complete gun assembly on its mount, with the cable counterbalance in place.

The more accurate elevation and traverse wheels were also from Alan's Grille. Styrene rod was used for the linkage.

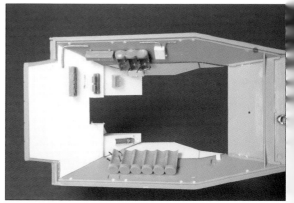

The upper hull, with all components in place prior to painting. The loose straps on the ammo containers are made from strips of thin lead foil and etched-metal buckles. The insides of the kit walls were thinned down with hobby knife and sandpaper.

In addition to the rear plate detail mentioned in the chapter on the early Hetzer, the external starter port was added by removing the kits moulded cover, and adding styrene tube and stiffeners.

The leaf-spring assemblies on the prototype vehicle featured the thicker frontal elements without the stiffening rib. The rear assembly had the rib, and both front and rear featured the hole below the leaf-spring housing. The lower parts had the kit's two large bolts removed, and six smaller ones added prior to painting.

The transmission and final drive area of the kit was detailed without adding anything that would be hidden behind the ammunition stowage box.

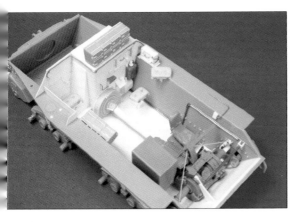

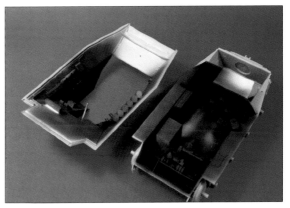

The general layout of the interior prior to painting.

The interior received a base coat of Floquil Dark-Brown paint.

The measurements for the armoured walls were determined by reference to a drawing in the book Ground Power no. 90 and the N.C. resin upper hull. The walls were cut from .015in. styrene sheet and taped in place to ensure correct fit and orientation. The top of the glacis was filed to the horizontal, unlike the resin representation that was perpendicular to the glacis. Before cementing the walls in place, the hull of the kit was thinned down from the inside at the point where the additional styrene was to meet it.

The weld beads were simulated using a couple of methods. Epoxy putty was rolled out to a thin strip and placed in position on the joint of the hull plate. A wooden toothpick with a carved convex end was 'jabbed' along the length, creating the desired texture. The length of a no. 11 X-acto blade was then used to remove the excess putty above and below the resulting bead. Working inside of the hull to create a similar effect, it was easier to take stretched styrene sprue and texture it after softening it with liquid cement.

A more accurate armour plate and spring were made for the underside of the gun, replacing the kit's resin parts. The spring was made by wrapping thin copper wire around a styrene rod, forming the 'tail' on which it rested.

The rear plate was modified to feature the uncovered starter port. The moulded cover on the kit part was removed with pliers and scraped flat with a

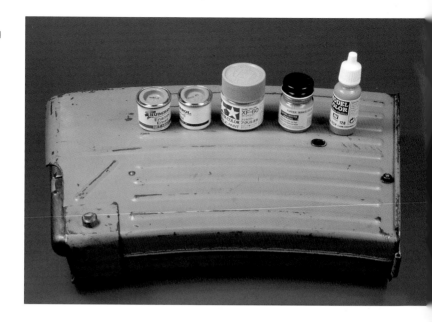

What colour is Dunkelgelb? A mixture of Tamiya acrylics was used to come up with a close match to this German 20mm magazine in its original finish.

The interior components, with their coat of Dunkelgelb and detail painting, prior to weathering.

no. 11 blade. The port was built up with two different sizes of styrene tubing, and fitted with small stiffening ribs and bolt heads.

The sIG 33/2 gun and platform

Due to detail and casting difficulties with the resin main gun, a styrene replacement was adapted. The front gun section from the Grille M kit by Alan was mated to the New Connection resin cradle. The cradle in the Alan kit is too short, while the resin part by N.C. features very good rivet detail and is the correct length. The Alan gun is more representative of the weapon, and it was given added detail to match pictures taken at the factory.

The counterbalance for the weapon incorporated the use of a cable and pulley system. To model this effectively, the entire gun and platform were constructed in one piece, and cemented into the lower hull before the upper and lower hull were joined.

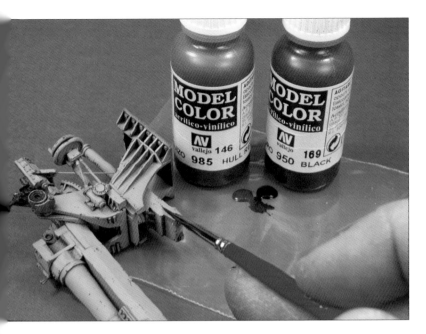

Paint chips were added to enhance the detail of the kit by mixing Vallejo Black and Hull Red together, thinned with water.

Scotch-Brite scouring pad material was used to cover general areas with scuffs and scrapes after dipping it into the paint and daubing it off on a piece of card to eliminate the excess.

Interior detailing – deciding the layout

The layout of the interior of the vehicle is a bit of a mystery, since the only known photos of this vehicle are ones from the outside taken at the factory. Since the firewall was reduced in height, the normal position for the Fu5 radio combination must have been changed. There was still room for one component in the firewall, and the second could have been close-coupled in the area immediately to the left above the sponson.

The sIG 33 gunner's seat had to be positioned for him to operate the elevation/traverse and look through the sight. After studying the placement of this seat in other vehicles (like the Grille H and K) and considering the room available, it was determined that the seat should sit on the sponson at an angle by the elevation/traverse control.

The positions for the loader and gunner. The radios were detailed using Vallejo paint, which is ideal for small touches like lettering and gauges.

The sIG 33 gun, ready for installation in the kit.

The ammunition detail set from Armo included brass base plates for the shells, which were glued in place over the holes in the ammo box to the right of the transmission.

With the sIG 33 in place, the drive shaft could be fed through the mount and cemented into position. The cramped conditions in this vehicle are evident.

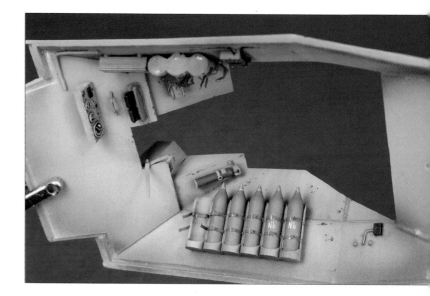

The ammunition was painted separately and added to the holders with lead foil straps. The shells marked with a 'Nb' were used for smoke.

After attaching the upper hull to the lower, gaps were filled with epoxy putty under the front mudguards and around the rear plate.

The kit's rear idlers have to be either replaced with the Model Kasten ones or have their shaft diameters increased to accept the resin wheels from Fort Duquesne. With a firm fit into the hull, the proper tension can then be put on the 96 track links.

A protective armour plate was added to the rear of the fighting compartment once the charge boxes had been positioned. Hinge detail on the rear plate had to be added using styrene scraps and bolt heads.

The armour plates around the gun were cut according to drawings, then test-fitted repeatedly to obtain the proper position.

The perforated guard around the silencer was formed around a piece of aluminium tubing, then positioned onto the silencer with four small blocks of styrene. The blocks were superglued under the locating bolts on the guard.

As with the late Hetzer, a firewall was built with .015in. styrene sheet and the resin engine drive housing glued in position. An earlier style of heater outlet was cut and cemented into place, along with accommodation for the radio receiver. A mount for the radio transmitter was built and positioned on the left sponson. There was just enough room to position an intercom box on the left wall just ahead of the transmitter.

A seat for the loader/radio operator was set in the same position as in the standard vehicle. The driver's position and steering and drive components were built in a similar fashion to the late Hetzer model, leaving out the detail behind the ammo stowage box as it was hidden from view. The N.C. steering arms and additional resin detail were exquisitely moulded in this area.

Since some of the kit's ammunition was moulded into their mounts, separate ammo was added to wall mounts from the Alan Grille M kit. The turned aluminium shells from Armo (kit no. 35 724) fitted nicely into the mounts. The more tapered alternatives provided in the same bag weren't a type used with the sIG 33. The shells were held in place with an upper and lower buckle and strap. These were replicated from lead foil and etched-brass details.

The vehicle track runs were painted a mixture of Humbrol enamel nos. 67 and 29. Enamel was used so that the subsequent use of acrylic thinner did not harm the paint.

Ground pastel chalk colours were mixed with Tamiya thinner and the colours blotted individually onto the track runs.

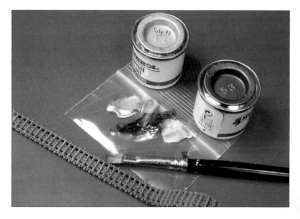

A mix of Humbrol Silver and Steel was brushed on to highlight the points of bare metal, avoiding a harsh look.

Dragging black pastel powder down the run between the guide teeth simulates the tyre marks.

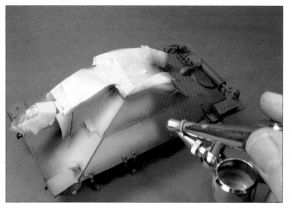

The interior components were masked off and a base of Floquil Dark Brown was sprayed on. After letting this dry for at least 48hrs, the model was then airbrushed by misting on the Dunkelgelb Tamiya mixture.

After all of the details had been painted a coat of thinned Tamiya acrylic dirt mixture was airbrushed onto the entire kit, concentrating on the lower areas.

A mix of Hudson & Allen Mud, pastel colour and water were dabbed onto the running gear and lower hull to give the effect of splashed mud. A second coat of this mixture, once Jo Sonja raw umber gouache had been added to it, simulated smaller amounts of wet mud.

Since the resin charge boxes for the ammunition were understated and warped, replacements from the Alan kit were substituted after they had been detailed with thin .010in. styrene stiffening ribs and fasteners.

Painting process

The model was primer coated with a Floquil mixture of Roof Brown and Engine Black. Serving two purposes, the lacquer paint gives a good 'tooth' to the subsequent acrylics, and the dark colour allows a pre-shade to the overall finish. With a significant amount of brass parts on the model, it is important that the surfaces of the finished kit are prepared by cleaning with vinegar and water solution before any paint is applied. Soap solution can also be used to rid the resin and styrene surfaces of any mould release residue.

Painting the interior

As with the late Hetzer, the painting process begins with the interior. Despite the period photos showing this vehicle to have a dark interior, this was attributed to shadow and thus the inside of the model was painted Dunkelgelb. After priming the interior components with the Floquil dark brown, it was allowed to dry for at least 48 hours. A Dunkelgelb colour was mixed from Tamiya acrylics to match

Washes of oil paint were applied to enhance some of the weld detail and other nooks and crannies.

wartime example acquired from a collector. A 20mm FlaK gun magazine was used as a colour guide, and a ratio of 4 parts Dark Yellow XF60 to 1 part Desert Yellow XF59 was used. The paint was thinned 50 per cent with Tamiya acrylic thinner, and misted onto the surface, allowing the darker primer to remain as shadow.

Allowing the base colour to dry overnight, the details were then picked out using Vallejo watercolours. Water-based paint was used so that the spirit thinner wash applied afterwards was less likely to attack the finish. The wash was applied an area at a time by soaking the surface with spirit-based clear paint thinner; a thinned raw umber oil paint was then applied to the detail to be enhanced. Judging the amount of thinning and the amount to load up on the 000 brush is a matter of experience, but it is best to go with a small amount first, and add more later if needed. Care is needed to ensure that no dark soak marks develop on the surface, and a clean brush dampened with thinner can be used to handle any mess. For a uniformly dirty look, all surfaces need to get the same wash treatment.

To give the interior surfaces and components a worn, chipped and scuffed look, small scratches were painted onto the components. The scratches not only weather the model, but also enhance the detail. Black, Hull Red and White Vallejo paint were combined and applied to the model in the appropriate spots with a very small pointy brush, keeping the effect random. Bare metal can be shown using a silver or graphite pencil sparingly so as not to overdo the effect. To give some larger areas of wear and tear, a Scotch Brite scouring pad can be used to apply the paint chips.

Since the interior will be enclosed and inaccessible at a later stage, any other dirt and weathering should be applied beforehand. Generally, crews would try and keep the fighting compartment as clean as possible, but evidence of some dust and dirt accumulation enhances the character of the model. The seat cushions, floor and transmission components were given a drybrushing of Humbrol Dark Earth no. 29 enamel. Earth-coloured pastel chalks were ground up on sandpaper and applied to various areas inside to make things look 'lived in'.

Painting the exterior

The exterior of the model needs to be painted just before the wheels are added. This is because the hull is easier to handle with the swing arms for the wheels firmly glued in place. The wheels were painted separately, along with the side skirts. The etched-brass skirts used on the model were left on the runner for

To make a faded and weather-beaten finish on a plain colour, small spots of oil paint were added in a random fashion.

To complete the effect, a brush dampened with thinner was lightly dragged down the surface, blending the paint into the finish.

The road wheels received a worn metal mark at the point of contact with the track using a silver pencil.

ease of handling. With all painted surfaces in the open-topped hull fully masked, the model was ready for the next step.

All components received the Floquil primer and base coat of Dunkelgelb Tamiya acrylic as described above. Again, details like the tools, tyres, spare track, and rear convoy light were painted afterward. Since there were no insignia or tactical markings on this subject, the next step was to airbrush on a coat of thinned acrylic dirt colour. Mixed from various Tamiya colours, it is important to keep this paint above 80 per cent thinner because the effect needed is subtle. Concentrating on the lower regions of the vehicle, the paint was misted onto all areas with an airbrush. All sub-assemblies, such as the wheels in this case, get the same treatment.

To add to the accumulation of muck that gets caught up under the vehicle, a mixture of Hudson & Allen Mud, pastel chalks and water was combined in a small metal pan and applied to the underside of the model. Care was taken to ensure the effect was random and not overstated. After the initial application, a second coat was applied with a slightly darker colour, indicative of wetter, fresher mud.

ABOVE The final addition to the kit was the antenna, which was taken from the DML set and carefully thinned down to a more realistic proportion with sandpaper.

BELOW Chipped paint and scratches were added to the exterior of the vehicle using Vallejo watercolours.

ABOVE The side skirts were painted on the etched-metal sprue to ease handling, and touched up later after assembly.

BELOW The engine deck area behind the commander's position was given some wear and tear by rubbing powdered graphite lightly over the finish. This was the only access for the crew, and the finish around it probably wore quickly.

The upper supports for the tow cable were canted inward. A folding step was added over the access hatch for the coolant heater.

Photos show the support bars for the spare track to be a darker colour than the vehicle, so they were picked out in red primer. The engine hatches were unlocked by loosening square-ended bolts located by the handles. These bolts were made from .020in. styrene.

The rivet detail of the sIG 33 gun and cradle was brought out by the washes of oil paint

The only known photos of this version of the Hetzer were of the prototype, taken at the BMM factory. The alleged 30 or so production vehicles were manufactured at Alkett in Germany.

One section at a time, the exterior of the vehicle received the raw umber oil paint wash. As before, each section was lightly soaked in spirit thinner, and a 000 brush was used to apply the thinned paint. The wash was dragged down the sides of the vehicle to simulate rain marks on the surface. This same technique was applied to the road wheels, which got more attention at the hubs. The wheel hubs show an accumulation of grease stains in reference photos, and adding a bit of black to the mix and dragging it out from the centre simulated the typical marks created.

To vary the appearance of a somewhat drab colour scheme, the model was treated to a technique using brown and white oil paints. Small dots of burnt sienna, raw umber and white oils were placed randomly on the model's dry surface and then blended into the paint scheme with a large brush moistened with thinner. The result was a partially faded, weathered look typical of a vehicle that has spent some time in the elements. Scrapes and scratches to the paintwork were then added in the appropriate spots, keeping in mind the causes – debris strikes from nearby explosions, wear and tear from the crew, and collision damage.

Painting the tracks

The tracks received a coat of Humbrol no. 29 Dark Earth mixed with no. 67 Dark Grey. It is important to use an enamel base since chalk pastels were added to the tracks using Tamiya acrylic thinner as a second stage, and this dissolves acrylic paint. After the track runs were dry, various pastel chalks in earth and rust colours were sanded off into small aluminium dishes, and added randomly to the lengths by mixing with the thinner. After this, Humbrol 53 Gunmetal and no. 11 Silver were mixed and drybrushed onto the raised detail of the track, which also blended the pastel colours.

Bergepanzer 38(t) and vignettes

Subject:	*Bergepanzer 38(t) and vignettes*
Model by:	*Gary Edmundson*
Basic kit:	*Dragon Models Ltd. 'Hetzer' Command Version kit no. 6060*
Resin conversion kit:	*New Connection Models Bergehetzer w. winch and spade, no. 35001*
Tracks:	*Friulmodel Hetzer track ATL-15*
Figures:	*DML Armoured Reconnaissance, Wiking Division (Hungary 1945) kit no.6131, Warriors SS Grenadier WA35014*

As a special feature, this chapter deals with constructing a recovery variant of the Hetzer, and placing it in a realistic setting. The Bergepanzer 38(t) model had been built a few years ago, and the steps to bring it up to standard will be covered. Two different diorama options are explored with the model being placed in both a rural and urban vignette.

Brief history

The recovery version of the Hetzer was produced by BMM in Prague, and 106 vehicles were built by the end of the war. The example modelled here was a specific vehicle produced in February 1945 that featured a large spade and winch for recovery operations. Two model companies produce kits of the Bergepanzer 38(t) in 1/35 scale: New Connections from Germany has a conversion set for the DML kit, and JP Hobby from the Czech Republic have a complete multimedia kit.

Bergepanzer 38(t)

The New Connections resin kit conversion models vehicle serial no. 322519 that was completed and photographed at the BMM factory in February 1945. Featuring a large spade on the rear, this test vehicle was very likely to be the only one so equipped. The model was constructed using the DML 'Command Version' Hetzer kit no. 6060 along with N.C. resin conversion kit no. 35001. The conversion kit came with details in white metal that are now thankfully produced in resin.

Running gear

For the most part, the model has the same running gear configuration as the late Hetzer. The 16-rivet roadwheels in this case were created by removing every second rivet from the 32-rivet style provided in the kit. Tracks used were the white metal Friulmodel early style – also early in that they are the original 'clamp' style before Friul came out with the pin type. The extravagant modeller may wish to add a few late-style Hetzer track links to the left-hand run, since photos indicate a mixture.

This vehicle had one peculiarity noted in few publications – the idler wheels were different styles on each side. The right side had the standard dished 6-hole pattern, whereas the left side had a dished 8-hole pattern with ribs in between. The left idler was made by casting two plain dish bases, drilling 8 holes in each, and adding styrene ribs for the inside and outside.

New Connections Bergepanzer 38(t) was designed to fit the DML Hetzer. Friulmodel tracks were fitted to the kit by trimming the bottoms of the road wheels to fit between the guide teeth.

The resin kit conversion featured white-metal parts at the time it was first released. Tool clasps on the jack were made of metal from an old tube of contact cement.

For those wishing to give this model the correct sit, the rear of the hull sat slightly lower than the front due to the weight of the spade.

Interior

The detail around the transmission and final drive should be constructed as per the late Hetzer and sIG 33 models. A bench seat was made from styrene and added behind the driver. The winch assembly, gear-driven from the transmission, sits at an angle and allows the cable to line up with the hole in the firewall. Although featured in this model, it is believed the leather pad to the left of the driver was a post-war addition to the later ST-1 and G13 vehicles and not used in the wartime Bergepanzer 38(t).

Hull details

The white-metal exhaust supplied by New Connections was too small and poorly shaped. I used the Dragon one and added a small bracket at the back to support it. The front end of the *Flamm-Vernichter* style exhaust was hollowed out, and Aber's brass detail used to support the pipe. My reference showed the exhaust pointing straight back from its point of exit from the engine deck.

The kit features a winch with linkage to the transmission.

With references being sparse, the interior was largely speculative. The bench seat behind the driver was built from styrene and given a cushion made of putty.

As an upgrade to the kit, a new idler wheel for the left-hand side was made using cast resin blanks. Eight holes were drilled, and small styrene ribs added.

The individual ribs were first positioned using liquid styrene cement, then fixed permanently with cyano glue.

The original towing pintles on the vehicle were cut off, and new ones welded on both the front and back of the vehicle in the form of steel loops. The ones at the rear appeared to be bigger than the ones on the front, so different size solder wire was used to make the corresponding changes.

The early-style driver's periscope cover provided on the resin hull needs to be removed, and the later one added using the modified kit part (remove the rain lip). Small hooks for the tarpaulin cover need to be cemented around the perimeter of the crew compartment.

The stowed pipes for the jib crane were given shackles for the ends. I made these out of aluminium strip from a disposable ashtray. Grant Line bolts were added to these items, and small retaining chains were added using a variety of photo-etched and miniature chains. The left front stowage rack also received a strengthening rib that appeared in the reference photos.

The more uncommon riveted side skirts were installed on the vehicle, so Grant Line rivet heads were added to the kit skirts to complete this detail.

Since the periscope cover was the later style, the early armoured style had to be removed with careful use of a Dremel tool.

Aber includes some nice detail for the *Flamm-Vernichter*. Some veterans claim that this style of exhaust was noisy, and alerted the enemy artillery as to their location.

Notes on painting and markings

Although Osprey's New Vanguard 36 depicts this vehicle in a brown and tan scheme, back in 1999 the model was painted with colours interpreted from the black and white wartime photographs. Assuming a Dunkelgelb base, seen on the lower front glacis, most of the body of the vehicle appeared a slightly darker shade (Olivgrün), with larger patches of a yet darker colour (Rotbraun). Thin lines of off-white (based on the appearance of the white no-smoking sign in the background) randomly snaked over smaller areas of the vehicle.

The model was airbrushed in Model Master enamel Panzer Olivgrün 1943, then brush-painted in a hard-edged scheme with Model Master Panzer Schokladenbraun, and Tamiya's acrylic Buff. The Dunkelgelb underside and running gear were airbrushed with Tamiya's Dark Yellow XF-60.

Two black bands were situated around the driver's periscopes, and were painted in the same fashion as on the late Hetzer. The serial number of the vehicle was applied to the glacis plate using small Letraset rub-on markings.

To incorporate the new modifications to the kit, the same jars of Model Master enamels used previously were painted on with airbrush and bristle.

Heavier weathering was added to the finish, incorporating the technique of a thinned Tamiya dirt colour being airbrushed on to the entire vehicle.

Pastel chalks were liberally applied to the large spade, followed in turn by 'metalising' the edges with a HB pencil.

The profile of the model shows the spade arms to be too thin. Stowed on the left-hand side were the components for the frame of the hoist. The side skirts were riveted to their supports as opposed to welded.

Black bands were featured on the glacis plate around the driver's visor, and a serial number was added using small Letraset rub-on numbers. The shackles for the hoist were made from soft metal strip and Grant Line bolt heads.

The vehicle sported a new design of towing pintle. The hull extensions were removed, and 'U'-shaped steel loops were welded to the lower front glacis and rear plate. This was modelled using thick solder wire.

To avoid interfering with the winch-cable bracket, the exhaust was positioned straight back, and not at an angle as on the standard Hetzer. The support bar for the spare track links was made with strip styrene.

The tow bars were given miniature retaining chains. The balsa post supplied in the New Connection's kit well simulates the roughly hewn look.

The BMM factory building

To give the models a realistic setting, a section of the factory building used as a backdrop for wartime pictures was reproduced in 1/35 scale. The ivy-covered structure is familiar to modellers of the Czechoslovakian vehicles, and recognisable with the cobblestone road in front, and the 'No Smoking' sign printed in both German and Czech.

Studying various views of the building, a rough sketch was drawn out on a piece of cardboard. The cardboard was placed behind a model to estimate how much of the structure to re-create, and get an estimate of the size needed for the proper camera angle for photographs.

Walls

After transferring the measurements onto a paper plan, windows, doors and other miscellaneous details were pencilled in. The main wall was to be 34cm long and 18cm high. The smaller wall measured 14.5cm long, and all of the windows were standardized at 5 x 3cm. The refined plan was then applied to .020in. styrene sheet, which was stiff enough to stand up to the required size of the walls. The walls were then cut out and the locations of windows and doors marked on the back.

Construction of the BMM factory façade starts with .020in. styrene card and some strip cut to make the various openings.

After the window and doorframes were cemented into place, the openings were cut out with a hobby knife allowing a small amount of excess to be trimmed later.

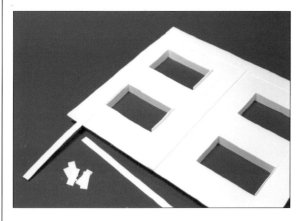

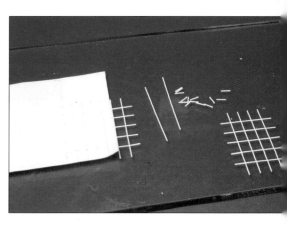

Detailing was added through studying photographs of the actual building, and adding the appropriate styrene strip where necessary.

Frames for the windowpanes were fashioned from .010 x .020in. Evergreen styrene strip. This was purchased, since attempting to cut your own only curls the pieces. The assemblies were done on glass with liquid cement, and removed with the help of a razor.

The completed building corner measured 34 x 14.5 x 18cm high.

The building was painted a greyish tan with Tamiya acrylics. White was added to the original colour, and the walls were highlighted to give a faded effect.

The building's 'No Smoking' sign, written in German and Czechoslovakian, was photocopied from a book, touched up with Vallejo paint and attached to a piece of styrene with a glue stick. To cover the walls with ivy, white glue was spread onto the surface in the appropriate areas.

Hudson & Allen Ivy was sprinkled onto the PVA glue with the excess falling into a newspaper to be gathered and re-used.

After cutting .015in. styrene into 8mm strips, pieces were cut with a chopper to make the window frames that were glued onto the back of the wall. The styrene remaining in the frames was carved out, leaving a spot for the windows to be inserted. Features on the face of the building were added with more styrene strip, in some cases textured with a lacquer-based paste product called Mr. Surfacer 500. After joining the two walls at 90 degrees, a top was measured for and cut from the .020in. styrene sheet.

The structure was given a coat of Tamiya acrylic paint mixed from a number of colours to give a drab mortar look. Tamiya Buff, Khaki Drab and Earth mixed with a bit of White were airbrushed on, after which a light dusting of thinned buff was sprayed in various areas to highlight the detail.

Windows

The window glass was made from ordinary overhead projector acetate sheet. Patterns for the individually framed panes were made from thin styrene strip,

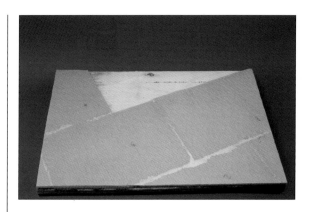

VP Productions cobblestone street sections were combined to fill out the base around the building. The resin sections are rather thick, and were cut with a coping saw.

After painting the base a light tan, it was washed with thinned black and brown oil paints. Matte board from a picture framing shop was cut and added to form the outside of the base, as well as provide a back for the building.

glued together onto a piece of glass, then lifted with a razor. The resulting pieces were airbrushed black, and then carefully tacked in place onto the clear acetate with white PVA glue. A double main entrance was added in a similar way. The windows and doorway were cemented in place with PVA glue after the structure had been painted.

Details

Rather than try to draw the 'No Smoking' sign by hand, a photo of the actual building wall was photocopied and adjusted to the right size. The sign was snipped out with scissors, retouched with paint, and mounted on a styrene base with a glue stick.

A couple of other small signs and a styrene rod drainpipe were added to the front wall. A light above the doorway was fashioned from styrene tube and brass rod. White markings on either side of the doorway were painted with an off-white Vallejo paint.

The most prominent detail to add was the significant growth of ivy on the wall. With reference to the wartime photos, the pattern of the ivy was copied with blobs of PVA glue, over which was sprinkled liberal amounts of Hudson & Allen ivy.

Base

Four Verlinden Products resin cobblestone sections were attached to a ³⁄₄in. plywood base and trimmed to fit around where the building was to be positioned. The resin was cut with a coping saw and filed to the correct contours with a wood rasp. The sections were joined together with cyano glue, and the gaps filled with epoxy putty. The cobblestone pattern was impressed into the putty to achieve a homogeneous appearance.

The roadway was airbrushed with a mixture of Tamiya acrylic paint to give a light tan appearance. Once dry, this was washed much the same as with the models using white spirit paint thinner and black and raw umber oil paints. This brought out the texture of the cobblestone detail.

The building structure was set into place, and a section of black matte board was cut to fit the rear. The same matte board was also cut as a surround for the base, following the contours of the slightly undulating cobblestones. PVA glue was used to fix these, ensuring that the cuts weren't visible from the front, and each section was sufficiently dry before the next one was added.

A small section of dirt and foliage was added to the building perimeter using model railway brick border and Celluclay paste. Hudson & Allen foliage (which

The factory building provides a historically accurate urban setting for the Bergepanzer 38(t)

consists of larger birch seedpods than the ivy product) was pressed into the pre-coloured Celluclay along with some small dried plant limbs.

The details on the building were enhanced with thinner and oil paint washes. The wash technique was also used to create rain streaks and other marks on the walls. The entire building and base was given a light dusting of thinned earth colour acrylic paint with an airbrush. This stops things from looking toy-like by preventing the individual components from standing out starkly against each other.

Vignette with figures

A natural setting is a simple and effective way to display an AFV model, and adding figures to it brings the scene to life. A lost grenadier is given directions from two crewmen in the Bergepanzer in this rural setting. Two of DML's figures from the Armoured Reconnaissance, Wiking Division (Hungary 1945) kit no. 6131 were modified to fit the model by repositioning the arms and legs. New resin heads replaced the DML ones, adding a more lifelike appearance. The grenadier on the ground is one of the earlier Warrior's resin figures, well sculpted with fine detail.

After deciding on the setting and how the figures are to be posed, an appropriate base was sized up. In addition to the plywood and matte board from the previous example, an old trophy plaque works just as well for a base. Styrofoam SM® was trimmed with a retractable utility knife, placed on the base and tested with the vehicle and figures for symmetry. Contours were marked out with a black marker, and the foam trimmed to the desired shape and attached to the base using white PVA glue.

With the edges of the base masked off, a papier-mâché product called Celluclay was mixed with raw sienna acrylic paint, white glue and water, and spread onto the base in a similar fashion to icing a cake. A drawback with the Celluclay is a tendency to shrink as it dries, so it is important to use the minimum amount, spreading it thinly. To cover the wet clay at the sides of the base one can add commercially available static grass, but spices like dill and thyme from the kitchen work well too.

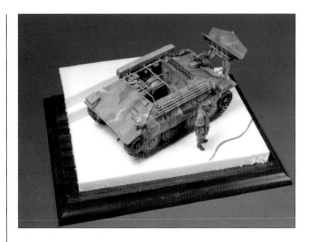

Cutting foam board into shape after positioning the model and figures as a guide starts a rural vignette.

Water, white glue and acrylic paint were mixed with Celluclay to form the groundwork on the contoured foam board.

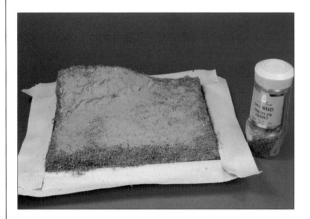

After spreading the clay onto the base, the edges were covered with Dill Weed spice. Although some spices tend to lose their colour with time, this type keeps its colour for longer.

Sand and grit were pressed into the wet mixture to form a path. It's important not to have any large pieces of gravel under the tracks of the vehicle in order to allow the model to sit properly.

Various colours of commercially available 'static grass' were sprinkled randomly onto the base, filling in open areas and adding some variety. To get the elements to stick, they were lightly prodded with a coarse paintbrush.

Hudson & Allen Tall Grass was snipped from its pelt, the tufts dipped into PVA glue, then positioned around the tree stump.

To form a dirt roadway, sand, grit and a bit of concrete dust were sprinkled on and patted into place in the wet clay. Various colours of static grass were placed on either side, with a small amount going up the middle of the road. Hudson & Allen's tall grass was then placed in patches on the rear bank; fishing shops sell a similar material for fly-tying, which is just dyed deer hair. To add a touch of interest, a broken tree stump was also glued into the bank after adding some of the Hudson & Allen dry product. After all of the groundwork was complete, the model and figure were pressed into the damp mixture to allow a proper sit once the base had dried.

A few words on photography

To further the enjoyment of plastic modelling, realistic pictures of the finished work can be taken. As a backdrop for vignettes and dioramas, one can use calendar pictures, purchase model railroad backdrops, or also find a spot outdoors that fits the scene.

Most of the pictures taken for this book were taken with an old Canon AT-1 35mm single lens reflex camera. The work was lit with four 500 watt daylight bulbs, positioned on tripods to move them around. The camera was set with an aperture of F22, which provided maximum depth of field. With these settings, the shutter speed had to be slowed down to $\frac{1}{4}$ or $\frac{1}{2}$ of a second, and a tripod mount and cable release were necessary. The film used was 100 ASA Fujichrome slide.

Figurines give a vignette life and perspective. These plastic figures are from a large line of DML releases, and were given detailed resin heads from Cromwell Models for a more animated appearance.

The model and figures were pressed into the damp base to allow proper 'sit'. The Celluclay shrinks as it dries, so the components won't eventually be as deep in the groundwork as they first appear.

ABOVE Outdoor photography can make the vignette appear quite realistic. The poor lost grenadier is a resin figure from Warriors Scale Models Inc., painted with Humbrol enamels

BELOW Photographs taken under diffused light tend to work better than in harsh sunlight. The model was pictured in overcast conditions in a local park with the camera set at F-22 and $\frac{1}{2}$-second shutter speed.

Further reading, media and websites

Books

Francev, V., Kliment C. K., and Kopecky M., *Hetzer Jagdpanzer 38*, MBI Publishing, 2001
An essential reference for building models of the Hetzer and its variants, this book has a very complete look at the subject from its inception to postwar use. Photos and illustrations are abundant, and it was an invaluable reference in preparing this publication.

Doyle H. L., and Jentz T. L., New Vanguard 36: *Jagdpanzer 38 'Hetzer' 1944–45*, Osprey Publishing, Oxford, 2001
In addition to the MBI book, this reference book is an affordable 'must have' for modelling the Hetzer. Included are condensed technical drawings of the Hetzer, which were enlarged on a photocopier and used as a main reference for the models in this book.

Jentz, T. L., *Panzer Tracts No. 9 Jagdpanzer*, Darlington Publications Inc., Maryland, 1997
Important technical information is contained in this book, the Hetzer being one of six types of Jagdpanzer described.

Kliment C. K., and Francev V., *Czechoslovak Armoured Fighting Vehicles 1918–1948*, Schiffer Military History, PA, 1997
This large hardcover book is the equivalent of the 'encyclopaedia' on Czech AFVs for the period.

Ground Power Number 089, Delta Publishing Company Ltd, Tokyo, 2001
This popular Japanese publication is the first in a series of three including many rare and detailed photos of the Jagdpanzer 38(t), the quality of which is superb. Included are the prototype, early, mid and late versions, along with numerous factory photos of the individual parts used in the construction of the vehicle.

Ground Power Number 090, Delta Publishing Company Ltd, Tokyo, 2001
Included in this volume are the Bergepanzer 38(t), sIG 33/2 version, Flammpanzer 38, Hetzer Starr, ST-1 and G-13.

Ground Power Number 091, Delta Publishing Company Ltd, Tokyo, 2001
Concluding the series with this volume, a photo study of the early Hetzer under restoration at Camp Borden in Canada is presented.

Jagd Model Fibel 1, Model Art Co. Ltd, Tokyo, 2001
A modelling special on German tank hunters, the first volume in this series starts with descriptive 'how to' builds on six different Hetzer models. Ranging from early to Starr variants, the book also features museum photos of the Bovington Hetzer and an ST-1.

Magazines

Model Graphix No. 1, Vol 111, Dai Nippon Kaiga Co. Ltd.

Zaloga, Steve, 'Hetzer of the Damned', *Military Modelling* Volume 29 No. 7, Nexus Publishing

Doi, Masahiro, '15cm sIG 33/2 (Sfl) auf Jagdpanzer 38(t)', *Armour Modelling* Vol.10,

Websites

http://www.pzfahrer.net/index.html
'A detailed study of the Jagdpanzer 38(t)' by Richard Gruetzner. This website is dedicated specifically to the vehicle, and includes many pictures and lengthy narratives on the Hetzer both during and after World War II. Links are provided to other websites that have related material, such as the Hetzer restoration project in Borden, Canada (http://www.geocities.com/Pentagon/6209/oct-hetz.htm), and military reenactment groups who own and run restored vehicles.

http://www.missing-lynx.com/
http://www.track-link.net/
http://www.ww2modelmaker.com/
These websites are devoted to AFV modelling. Their galleries contain photos of modellers' work to a high standard. Several discussion forums provide place where modellers and other enthusiasts to obtain and share information. The Missing Links website has had members compile a number of lists of specific kit modifications, including one on the Hetzer. These 'Tweak Lists' can be found at http://missinglinks2.tripod.com/index.htm.

Museums and collections

CFB Borden Military Museum, Borden, Ontario, Canada
The museum at Worthington Park is at the time of writing restoring a rare early version of the Hetzer captured by Canadian troops in Northwest Europe.

Aberdeen Proving Ground Ordnance Museum, Aberdeen, Maryland, USA
A large collection of vehicles at the APG in Aberdeen includes one of the final versions of the Hetzer taken back to the US for evaluation from the Skoda factory at the end of the war.

The Tank Museum, Bovington, Dorset, England
The Tank Museum acquired their 'late' Hetzer after it was captured and evaluated in the closing phases of the war.

The Swedish Tank Museum, Axvall, Sweden
The Swedish Tank Museum displays two examples of Hetzers, one a G-13, and the second an original early type from 1944.

Located at Camp Borden in Ontario, Canada, this early Hetzer was captured by Canadian troops and brought back for evaluation. It is currently undergoing restoration by the Worthington Park Museum. (Ron Volstad)

...e Military Technical Museum, Prague, Czechoslovakia
...e Lasany Museum near Prague displays a ST-1 and an original Hetzer used in ...e May 1945 uprising.

...itary History Museum of Armoured Vehicles and Equipment, ...binka, Russia
...wartime Hetzer with the later mantlet and sheet metal periscope cover is in ...e Russian tank collection housed in Kubinka.

...uzeum Wojska Polskiego, Warsaw, Poland
...uzeum Wojska Polskiego has on outdoor display a heavily damaged early ...etzer.

...usée des Blindés, Saumur, France
...e Hetzer example at the Musée des Blindés is a G-13, painted up to look like ...late-war Hetzer. Like many other vehicles at this museum, it is a 'runner'.

...e-enactment groups
...ere are several re-enactment groups around the world who collect and ...store military vehicles and equipment. Many have acquired G-13 'Hetzers' ...hich are modified to resemble the wartime vehicles.

...rivate collections
...FV collections of Jacques Littlefield of the USA and Kevin Wheatcroft of the ...K include post-war Hetzers restored to running condition. Hans Halberstadt ...atured the Littlefield vehicle in the book *Inside the Great Tanks*, which was ...sed as reference for this project.

Taken from the Skoda manufacturing facility and shipped back to the USA at the end of World War II, the Armour Proving Ground at Aberdeen, Maryland, has been the home for this Hetzer ever since. Having first been on display indoors, the vehicle has sat outside for decades and is showing the signs of heavy deterioration.

Kits available

Italeri 1/35-scale 'Hetzer' Kit no. 209
The kit, released in the mid-1970s by Italeri, makes into a fairly good late mode[l] with some improvements to the detail. The kit tracks are the vinyl band type but the kit is good value for the price. The overall quality of the kit is poo[r] compared to today's standards.

Cromwell Models 1/15-scale resin Hetzer
Released in 1993, this large kit is well-detailed, heavy, and available from Cromwell for £145! The kit is made up of all resin pieces. An impressive mode[l] when complete due to it's size, it represents a later production Hetze[r]. Drawbacks of the model are the rear plate which is at too steep an angle, givin[g] the kit an odd look; the leaf-spring housings are misshapen requiring a rebuild.

Dragon Models 1/35-scale Hetzer 'Early Version' DML 6030
DML's first kit of the Hetzer to be released came as a welcome addition to th[e] 1/35-scale AFV market. With technical research by well-known modelle[r] Thomas Anderson, the kit broke new ground in accuracy and detail. The mode[l] featured the early engine deck without the small access hatches at the back fo[r] the glycol and oil, and it is representative of a May–June 1944 productio[n]

Although it's about 30 years old, Italeri's 1/35-scale Hetzer kit is still available. The author built this model in 1988.

Cromwell Models 1/15-scale Hetzer is a large, heavy kit. David Parker's build of the review kit was featured in Military Modelling magazine's September 1993 issue. (David Parker)

model. Although DML's policy of providing individual link tracks continued with this release, the tracks provided were of the later design. Etched-metal components were also included in the kit, giving the modeller the engine outlet air screen and damper, and the silencer guard. Out of production for a while, this kit has now been re-released.

Dragon Models 1/35-scale Hetzer 'Mid Version/Flammpanzer' DML 6037
Although billed as a 'Mid', this kit builds into what would be called a late version based on modifications made after September 1944. Also included are the extra bits and pieces to construct one of 20 vehicles converted to flame-throwing duties. The model shares the same advantages of the 'early', being technically well designed and produced.

Dragon Models 1/35-scale Hetzer 'Command Version' DML 6060
Since this kit combined parts from both the early and late DML models mentioned above, it is the best one to purchase as far as flexibility is concerned. In addition to the added parts to make the command version, early and late mantlet and *Kugelafette*; engine decks; rear plates; silencers; and two different sets of road wheels are included. To make the deal even sweeter, DML threw in their panzer crew figure set. This model was used to make the Bergepanzer 38(t) featured in this book, but unfortunately at the time of writing the kit is out of production.

JP Hobby 1/35-scale Bergehetzer 38(t). no. JP35C01
Includes resin cast parts, photo-etched details and decals.

JP Hobby 1/35-scale s.I.G. 33/2 auf Jagdpanzer 38(t). no. JP35C02
Includes resin cast parts, photo-etched details, aluminum barrel and decals.

Fujimi 1/76-scale Hetzer. Kit 76003

Esci 1/72-scale Hetzer. Kit 8375

An accurate replica of the vehicle can be built with this kit, which comes wi[...]
link and length tracks. One drawback to the kit is the unclear instructions, a[...]
the fact that Esci has mis-numbered some of the parts. Unfortunately these k[...]
are currently out of production.

Available accessories in 1/35 scale

Verlinden Productions Hetzer Interior Cat. No. 1692

The VP Hetzer interior was designed around reference from the Littlefie[...]
Collection Hetzer featured in the book *Inside the Great Tanks*. Since the vehic[...]
is a postwar G-13 with a StuK 40 gun, numerous modifications are needed [...]
replicate a wartime vehicle interior featuring the Pak39/L48.

Verlinden Productions Hetzer Engine and Compartment Cat. No. 1097

Excellent detail is featured in this offering, although it represents a very la[...]
war configuration as regards the air filters.

JP Hobby Hetzer Detailed Engine Compartment for DML/Dragon JP35A09

Aber Detail Set Early Hetzer no. 35112
Aber Detail Set Late Hetzer no. 35113
Aber Hetzer Fender Set no. 35114

Aber's brass detail sets for the Hetzer follow their tradition of providing eve[...]
piece needed to replicate the vehicle down to the last nut and bolt. Researc[...]
and accuracy are evident in these sets offered, although a lot of the pa[...]
would not be considered an upgrade to the kit due to the limitations of th[...]
technology used in their production.

Royal Model Hetzer pt. 1 RM116 (brass and resin details)
Royal Model Hetzer pt. 2 RM117 (brass side skirts)
Eduard photo-etched detail set no. 35343 (for the 1/35-scale Italeri kit)
Eduard photo-etched detail set no. 35385 (for the DML kit)

The Royal Model and Eduard etched-metal details are not as elaborate as th[...]
Aber ones, but they do include the mudguards, which Aber offers separately.

An example of aftermarket accessories available for the 1/35-scale kits, the Aber etched-brass detail set for the early version Hetzer contains a wealth of parts.

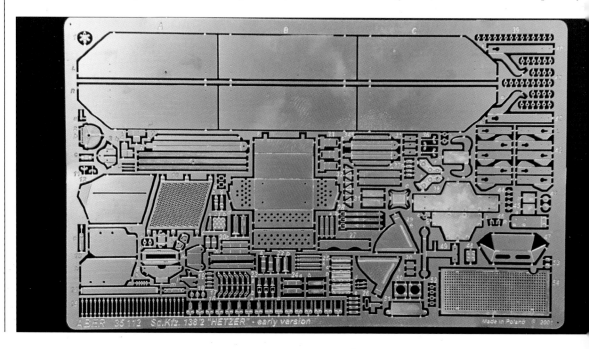

Model Kasten Early Hetzer Track Links SK-28
Model Kasten Late Hetzer Track Links SK-29
Friulmodel Early Hetzer Track Links ATL-15
Friulmodel Late Hetzer Track Links ATL-35
Both the Model Kasten and Friulmodel tracks are well designed and produced, and are an upgrade to the DML kit tracks.

Fort Duquesne Miniatures early Hetzer roadwheels FDA 104
Fort Duquesne Miniatures late Hetzer roadwheels FDA 105
R&J Enterprises early Hetzer roadwheels RJ35219
R&J Enterprises late Hetzer roadwheels RJ35220
JP Hobby late Hetzer roadwheels JP35A08
Chesapeake Model Designs late Hetzer roadwheels
These resin upgrades give the inside detail on the wheel hub and rim. Caution should be exercised when choosing the replacements, since some of these aftermarket wheels don't look the part.

Moskit Exhaust pipe for Hetzer SdKfz 138/2 no. MOS-3533
Flamm-Vernichter style Exhaust.

Resin conversion kits

MR Modellbau Hetzer Pre-production type MRA3526
Resin conversion kit for the prototype vehicle, includes an accurate rendition of the six-bolt *Kugelaffette*, ram's-horn tow hooks, flattened front leaf springs, and the initial drive housings.

New Connections conversions (for DML kit)
Bergehetzer w. winch and spade, no. 35001
sIG 33 on Hetzer, heavy infantry gun, no. 35002
Hetzer with 2cm FlaK 38 (recce), no. 35024
Hetzer with 7,5cm KwK L/24 (recce), no. 35025
JagdPz. 38 (t) Starr, no. 35027
Kätzchen (kitten) late war APC based on Hetzer, no. 35058
Hetzer Aufklärer (recce) / 2cm Hängelafette, no. 35062
Hetzer Pz.IV Turm / PAW 600, no. 35063

Index

1. Dunkelgelb

2. Olivgrün

3. Red primer

4. Red brown

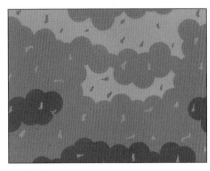

5. BMM ambush scheme

6. Early sprayed scheme

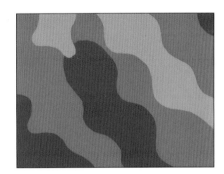

7. Skoda late-war scheme

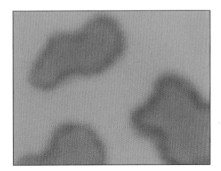

8. Sprayed cloud scheme

5. BMM ambush scheme

Jagdpanzer 38(t)s produced at the BMM factory in the summer of 1944 left the factory with a carefully applied camouflage pattern of cloud-like shapes, with small patches of colour added. The Skoda factory also produced vehicles in a similar 'ambush scheme' finish, with subtle differences.

6. Early sprayed scheme

The camouflage pattern featured on the early Hetzer in this book is from a colour plate in Osprey's New Vanguard 36: *Jagdpanzer 38(t) 'Hetzer' 1944–45*. The vehicle dates from May 1944, and was painted in the field.

7. Skoda late-war scheme

Hetzers at the Skoda plant at the end of the war featured a wavy, hard-edged camouflage pattern. The late Hetzer model is painted to resemble the example in Aberdeen Maryland based on a colour photo of the vehicle in *German Tanks Of World War II In Colour* published by Motorbooks International.

8. Sprayed cloud scheme

One of many various patterns of colour painted onto the Hetzers during their short existence. A vehicle numbered '233' knocked out on the Western Front featured these patches of green with a red brown outline sprayed over the Dunkelgelb base. A colour plate and photograph of the vehicle is featured in Francev's *Hetzer* by MBI.

1. Dunkelgelb

As of February 1943, German AFVs left the factory in a Dunkelgelb base paint, RAL 7028. Hetzers produced until the summer of 1944 were shipped in only the dark yellow base, and field units applied their own camouflage patterns using separately supplied tins of green-brown paste. The Dunkelgelb colour used on the models is a combination of Tamiya's XF-60 Dark Yellow and XF-59 Desert Yellow, mixed with a 4:1 ratio. This ratio was determined with reference to an original piece of equipment. There is variation in tone when applied to different base colours on the models.

2. Olivgrün

Applied to German AFVs as part of the three-colour camouflage pattern, this colour later became a base colour for a short period late in 1944. Hetzers had Olivgrün included in their paint scheme, either sprayed on or applied by brush. Testor's Model Master Acrylic and Enamel Panzer Olivgrün paints were used on the models.

3. Red primer

Red oxide primer, painted on as a preservative undercoat, became part of the three colour scheme and a base colour for German AFVs late in the war. Vehicle interiors also ended up leaving the factory in this finish, having previously been coated with an ivory colour. The floor, engine compartment, and base of the late Hetzer model were finished with this colour. Vallejo Cavalry Brown, Hull Red, and Flat Red were combined to match a primer example from a piece of *Zimmerit*.

4. Red brown

In combination with the Olivgrün, red brown (RAL 8017) was applied in spray and brush form on the vehicles as part of the three-colour scheme after February of 1943. Tamiya's Red Brown XF-64 was mixed with their black XF-1 to obtain an acrylic match to Model Master's Schokladenbraun enamel.